LEARN OR DIE

The New American Revolution

MARCELLO TINO

Conceptualization of Artwork
Marcello Tino and Andrea Dalla Bona
Illustrations by Andrea Dalla Bona

Learn or Die: The New American Revolution

ISBN: 978-0-578-79993-3

The Library of Congress Control Number: 1-9460190351
Thompson and Prince, Ithaca, NY

Key Words: American History, Politics, Economics, Political and Economic Theory, Democracy, Direct and Participatory Democracy, Capitalism, Free Market Capitalism, Globalism, Socialism, Anarcho-syndicalism, Mondragon, The New Deal, Neoliberalism, Co-determination, Mondragon, Revolution, The Federal Reserve, International Monetary Fund, World Bank, World Trade Organization, Economic Democracy, Political Democracy.

Logo designed by William Benson
Illustrations by Andrea Dalla Bona
Book designed by www.Delaney-Designs.com

Thompson and Prince

Distributors: Amazon.com, Ingram Book Company, Baker & Taylor

TABLE OF CONTENTS

Author's Note

Learn or Die: The New American Revolution is a traditional study in the social science in the sense that the thesis is supported by thorough research, facts, data, reason, and logic. However, unlike most studies, *Learn or Die* has a heartbeat and journeys beyond reason to find meaning in the metaphors and images that reveal the human condition in all its multiplicity and mystery. *Learn or Die* is about you and me and about our children. It is about our hopes and dreams and the horror that America has become.

To highlight the fact that beyond the numbers and the data and the T accounts that they crucify us on there is a heartbeat, I created Charlie and Daisy. Charlie and Daisy are near the end of their life. Charlie fought in the Second World War and was awarded a Silver Star. Charlie is an ordinary man who like most ordinary people was capable of doing extraordinary things in extraordinary times. After the war, Charlie did what so many Americans did who lived through the abject poverty of the Great Depression and the horrors of the Second World War, he embraced romantic love. Charlie and Daisy have been together ever since, for better or worse.

Now, at the end of their life, they are lost. The home they took pride in is in disrepair, and Charlie's truck is rusted out. They worked hard all their lives, sometimes two jobs to make ends meet, and they have nothing to show for it. Daisy and Charlie do not have much hope of being new again, but what they fear the most is not their own future. They fear for the future of their children and their grandchildren. The America Dream seems dead for them, and they wonder, what happened to us? What went wrong.

Learn or Die: The New American Revolution is, in part, Charlie and Daisy's journey through the labyrinth of illusions and lies that keep us from the truth that will gore us all, but through the handwriting on the wall, they begin to understand where we have been, where we are now, and where we must go if we ever hope to get back to America again.

Beware!

Illustration #1

PART ONE: Learn or Die

Vampires are Real

Vampire Capitalism – The Horror Story

There is no mystery to why stories about vampires and the living dead are so popular in the United States. They are true stories about a horrible reality that we are too afraid to face except as harmless fantasies filtered through our mass media. Even the Vampires of Capitalism can't face their true image in the mirror. They have to distance themselves from the monstrous reality they create, and they are supported in their avoidance of the bloody truth by an army of for-hire-professionals who have bared their necks to their masters so that they too can feed off of the body politic and the host nation.

Illustration #2

Trickle Down Blood

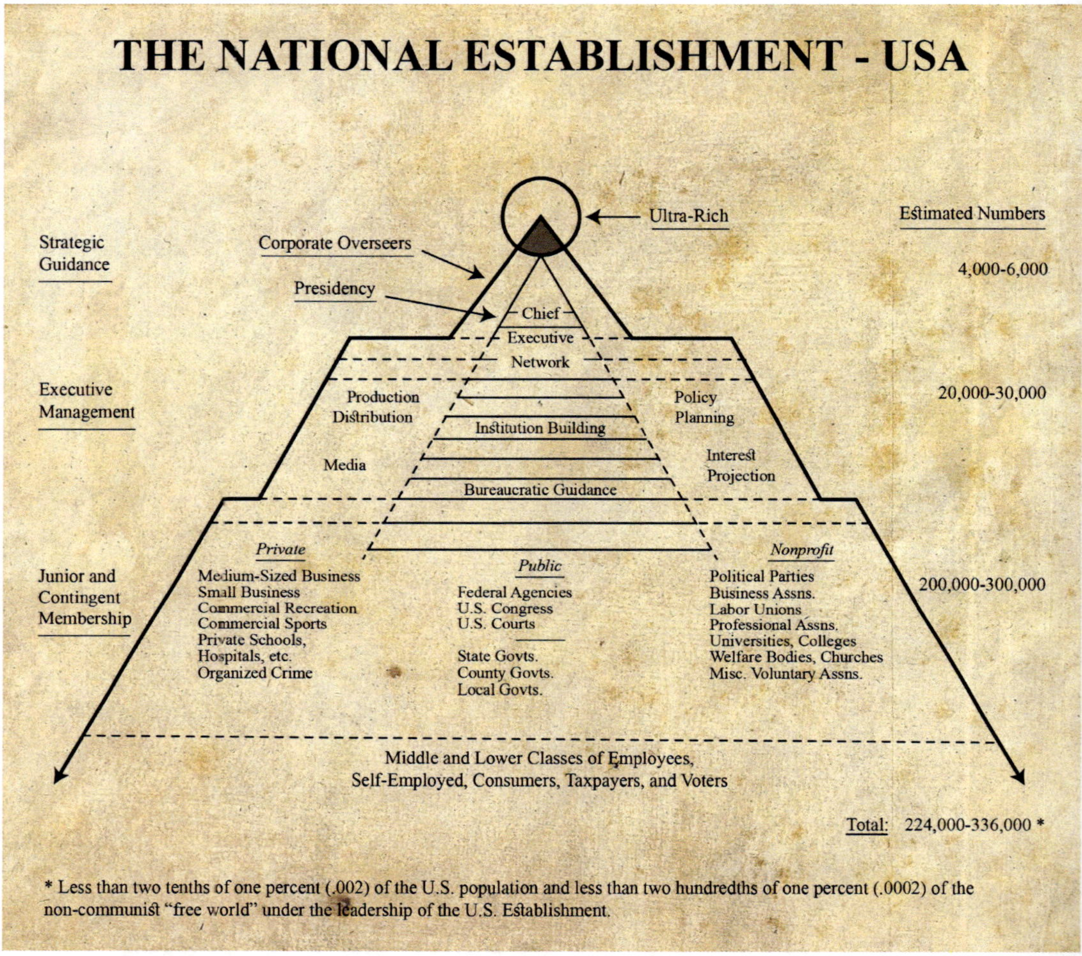

Illustration #3

As the above pyramid chart from Bertram Gross's book *Friendly Fascism* indicates, at the apex of the pyramid are the Ultra Rich and the Financial and Corporate Overseers. Included in this oligarchy of power is the President of the United States and those who assist him in his role as Commander-in-Chief and Chief Executive. The institutions and so-called experts responsible for making certain that the vast majority of blood flows to the top are centered around the Treasury Department, the Federal Reserve, the International Monetary Fund, the World Trade Organization, the World Bank, and the leading Wall Street bankers, especially the investment banks. All these financial institutions both domestic and international are supported by the pundits-for-hire at Harvard, MIT, and the MBA programs that train the corporate and the banking elite. As important are the hidden persuaders, the Madison Avenue advertisers and sellers of primitive totems that have turned every value, every virtue, and everything we have ever fought for including our democracy into a bad ad and a consumer-product-for-profit. Another major player in this horror story is the global media that create the stories that give our life meaning and value. (Gross 56)

They all wear a mask of respectability, but their job is to rationalize the irrational, sell us fairy tales of meaning, and abstract our pain and suffering by turning us into money, millions and billions of dollars that become electronic impulses on a computer screen, a far cry from the beating hearts of the victims of Vampire Capitalism. But make no mistake.

Money is Blood.

It is our life blood, our hopes and dreams, our children's futures that circulates through the veins of the body politic as currency. No matter how much the so-called economic experts try to hide the truth behind obscure mathematical formulas that give the illusion of science, and no matter what they call it – "neoliberal economics," "monetarism," or "supply side economics," – it is still the same old classic conservative free market economics that led us to the First Great Depression, nearly brought us to a Second Great Depression in 2008, and will bring America to a total economic collapse in the future. It is still the same old absurd gospel preached by the ministers of the God of Money, and the gospel goes like this - If we all pursue our own individual greed, we will somehow through the "invisible hand" of free market capitalism end up in Paradise.

This is not Paradise that we are going to. We are going to Hell, and as we descend into capitalist Hell, we see the emergence of the totalitarian state in America with a one-dollar-one-vote electoral system. We see a new aristocracy emerging in America of inherited wealth and power supported by a professional class who view themselves as part of a meritocracy in a nation that has little or no social mobility. So, where are we in this horror story?

Illustration #4

The Living Dead - Social Mobility in the United States

Social Mobility in the United States

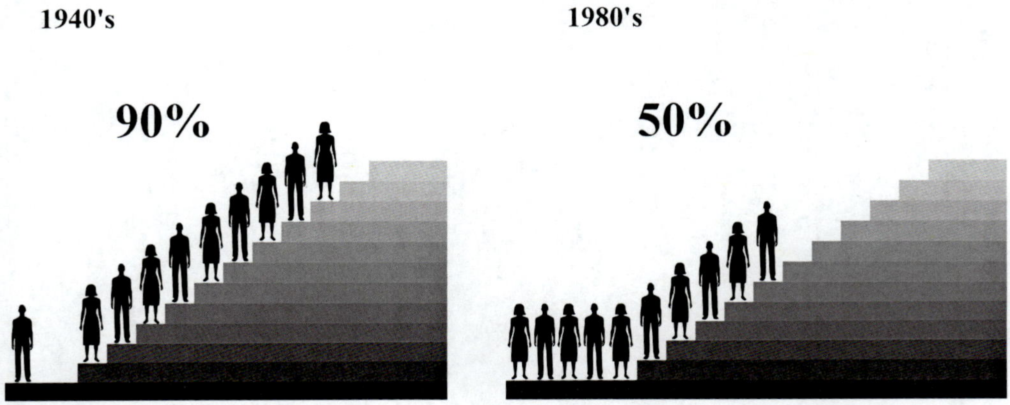

Chart #1

The above is an infographic conveying the results of research into social mobility in the United States by Raj Chetty. It reveals that the probability of children attaining a higher income than their parents has dropped dramatically in the United States from more than 90% for children born in 1940 to 50% for children born in the 1980s.

> The fact is that social mobility in the United States is a myth. The United States has less social mobility than any other developed country in the world except the United Kingdom and Italy who are close behind us. The countries with more social mobility include Demark, Australia, Norway, Finland, Canada, Sweden, Germany, Spain, France, Japan, New Zealand, Singapore, and even Pakistan. (Noah) I repeat.

Social Mobility in America is a Myth!

Illustration #5

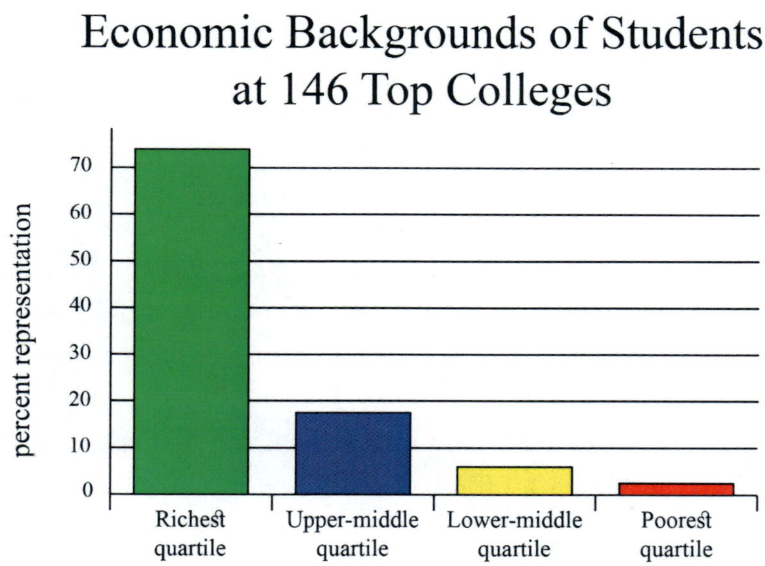

"America's Untapped Resource: Low-Income Students in Higher Education". Century Foundation Press, 2004.

Chart #2

Income Inequality in the United States

The United States not only has the lowest level of social mobility in the industrial world. It has the highest levels of income inequality. The poorest fifth of our population enjoy only 3.4% of the national income, while the richest fifth enjoy 50.3%.

> Another way of saying it is that the richest 20% of the population in the United States has as much income as the remaining 80% of the population, and over the last 10 years 80% of the increases in income in the United States have gone to the top 20%. Or in other words, if we were to create a scale where the height of a man is calculated based on the average income of $55,000 and the person with that income was 6 foot tall, the poorest 8 million people with an income of $9,000 dollars or less would be 1 foot tall, and the richest few with an income of $4.5 billion would be 90 miles high, higher than Mt. Everest! (Schweickart 90)

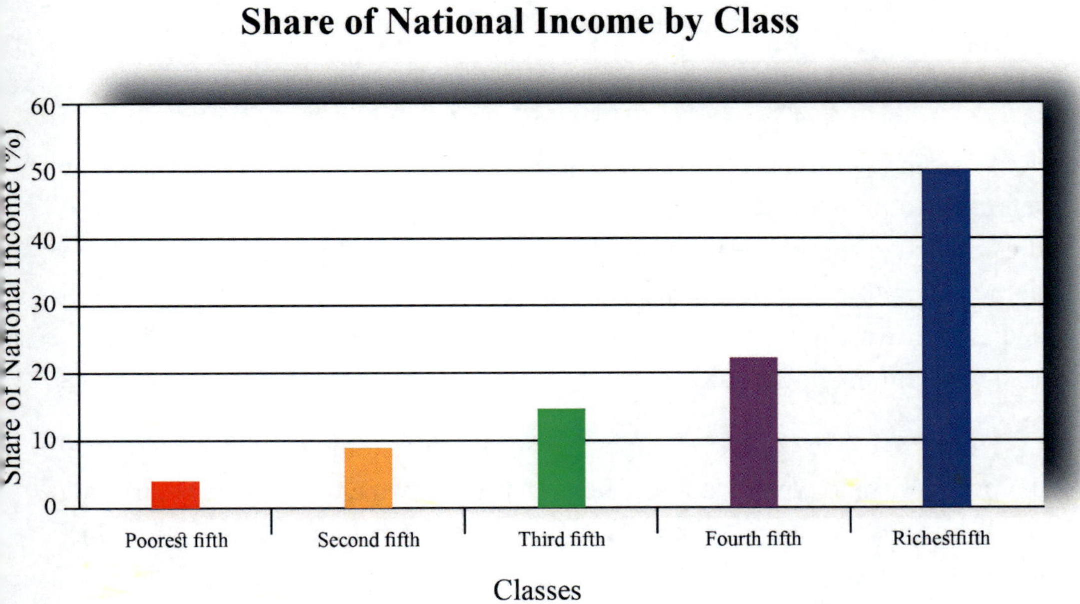

Chart #3

The chart below demonstrates that not only does the United States suffer from gross income inequality, but it also has the highest levels of income inequality in the industrial world.

Ranking of the United States in Income Inequality

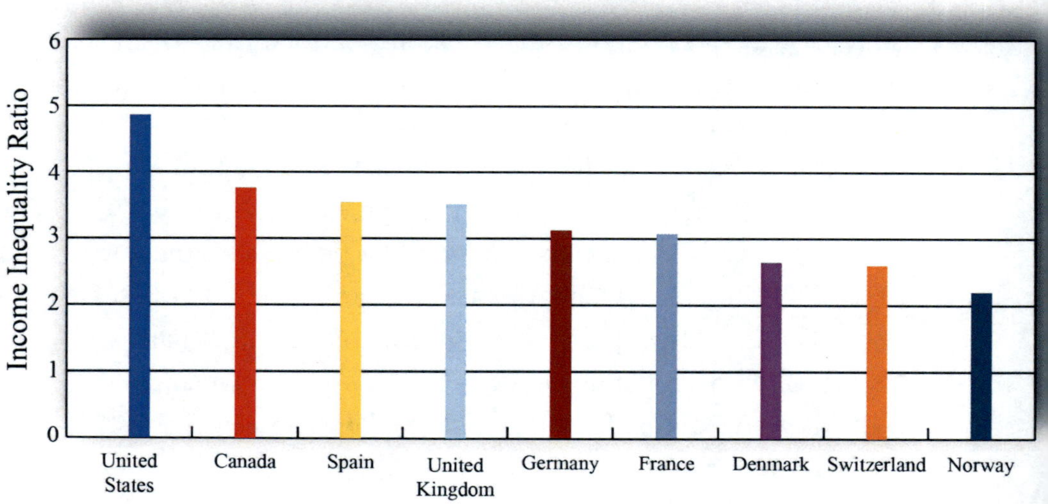

Chart #4

Wealth Inequality in the United States

For our purposes, in economic terms, when we refer to wealth, we are referring to net worth or the value of assets owned minus the value of liabilities owned at a point in time. Assets refer to personal property such as your home and automobile less what you owe on them as well as monetary savings and capital wealth such as real estate, stocks, bonds, and the net worth of any business you may own etc.

As of 2013, the top 1% (upper class) of households owned 36.1% of all the privately held wealth, and the next 19% (the managerial, professional, and small business stratum) owned 52% of all the privately held wealth, which means that just 20% of the people in the United States own an astounding 89% of all the privately held wealth in the nation leaving 11% of the wealth for the bottom 80% who live pay check to pay check.

Illustration #6

The Distribution of Financial Wealth in the United States

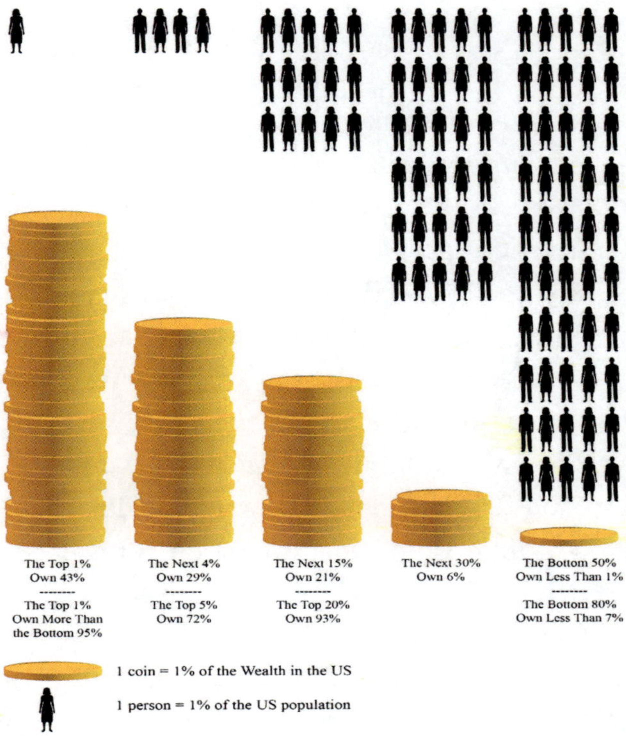

Chart #5

If US Land Was Divided Like US Wealth

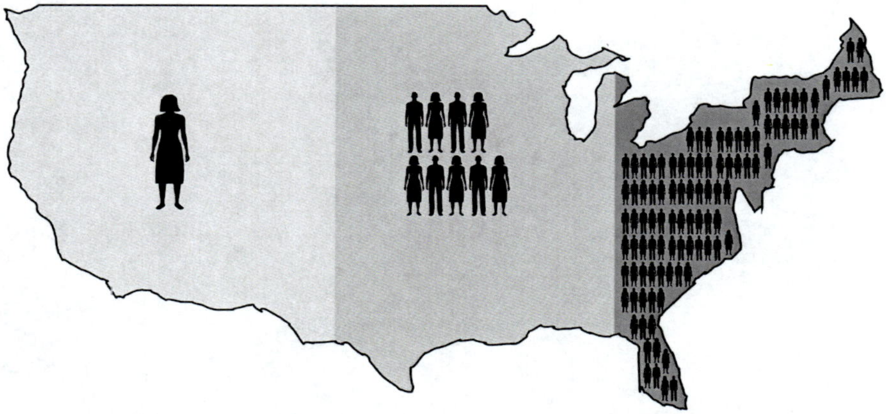

The Top 1%
Would Occupy 43%

The Next 9%
Would Occupy 40%

The Bottom 90%
Would Occupy 17%

Chart #6

The fact is that 10% of the American people own this country!

Very few Americans know that we have the highest levels of income and wealth inequality of all developed countries in the world, and, at the same time, have the lowest levels of social mobility. Very few Americans know that 10% of the American people own this country. For example, a study by (Norton and Arealy 2010) reveals that Americans have no idea how much wealth is concentrated on the top. When they were shown three pie charts that represented three different distributions of wealth, 90% or more of the 5,522 respondents – whatever their gender, age, income level, or party affiliation – thought that wealth distribution in the United States most resembles the pie chart in which the top 20% has about 60% of the wealth where, in fact, the top 20% control 89% of the wealth. Americans from all walks of life were also united in their vision of what the "ideal" wealth distribution would be, one in which the top 20% owned between 30 and 40% of the privately held wealth which is radically different than the 89% that the top 20% actually own. The American people are far more equitable in their vision of America than the Madison Avenue vision of an acquisitive society would lead us to believe.

Below is a chart illustrating the discrepancies.

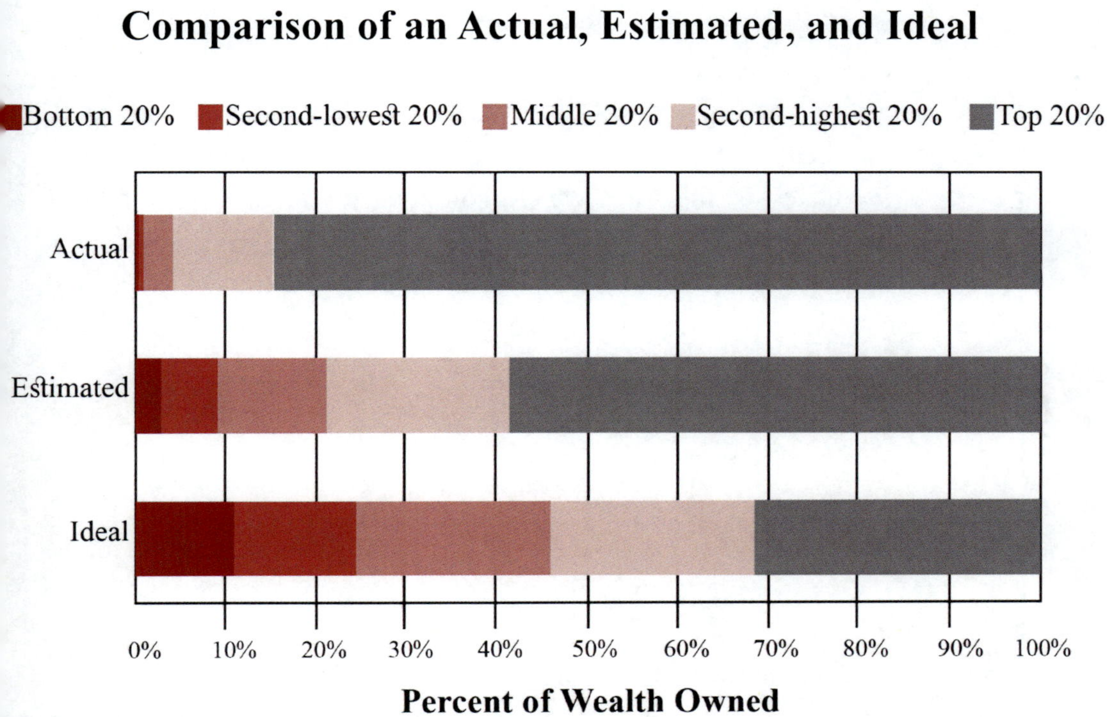

Chart #7

We Need to Wake Up!

We have no job security, nor can we look forward to a day that we can retire and reap the benefits of a life of hard work. Pensions are something of the past for most Americans. Our saving and social security are inadequate, and our children face a life of work until they die, while at the same time, we see a partnership of state capitalism and neo-fascism, a marriage in hell, characterized by (1) a contempt for democracy, (2) a glorification of the nation-state and imperial wars, (3) a perverted sense of manhood and a twisted concept of Social Darwinism that takes pleasure in inflicting pain and suffering on the innocent, (4) a regression into primitive forms of tribalism, racism, and brutality, (5) and an amoral economic system where it is a virtue to take more than you give. The results are staggering when we view it from the perspective of American history and what we have fought and died for.

We Lost the American Revolution

"The price of liberty is eternal vigilance," those words by Thomas Jefferson ring true today probably more than they ever have since our first revolutionary war because with the elimination of estate taxes, the creation of "dynasty trusts", and the accumulation of vast amounts of wealth and power in the hands of the few, we have lost the American Revolutionary War that we fought in 1775 against the oppression of a privileged aristocracy and the corporations that owned America as a franchise from the king, and with the rise of racism and neo-fascism in America, we have also lost the American Civil War and the Second World War. I repeat.

We have not only lost the American Revolution, but we have also lost the American Civil War, and the Second World War!

Where are the Americans who fought and died by the millions throughout our history, throughout the world believing that they fought for democracy, a nation of the people, by the people, and for the people, a promise, in fact, never fulfilled, a dream shattered by the vampire capitalist and their minions who have destroyed the American Dream and turned it into a nightmare. However, the greatest horror of all is that we have embraced our oppressors, embraced the fairy tales that we are told by the corporate controlled media that glorifies selfishness, narcissism, and wallows in sadomasochism and enjoys inflicting pain and suffering on the weak, the innocent, and the vulnerable.

> We allow ourselves to be sacrificed on the Alter of Money where we are dissected while we are still alive. We are turned into objects, body parts, hired hands, eyes to supervise. The faculties of our minds are compartmentalized to perform specific functions while the rest of our mind is left to die. Even our mouths are separated from our brains, and we are programed to year after year to say the same things over and over again. "Thank you, thank you, thank you," we say. "Have a good day," we say. "Yes, sir," we say, when you really want to say, "Fuck you!

I've had enough of this!" But we don't. Out of fear we bare our necks. Often, we do so just to survive on a minimum wage or less, often at the expense of working two jobs, just to stay above the poverty line with both parents working. We have no time to properly raise our children or simply go to our child's baseball game. There is no vacation time except for alcohol and drugs, so we take our vacation from the truth, and we enjoy the illusion of feeling good, like a cancer patient on his death bed, but we wake of the next day and the next day, year after year; we wake up and go to work in a totalitarian state that we called the "workplace" run by the bosses where we have no rights or freedoms and there is no escape, at least for us. So, we sacrifice for our children, and they go off to college. We all hope that this will mean that they will have a better future, only to see them come home after graduation owing so much money to the banks that they have become indentured servants for most of their lives.

This is not the American Dream, but this is the America we live in today. It is a horror story that has come true, a horror story where every human value is left silent before the God of Money. Every human value that in a civilized society is viewed as having a value in itself or is viewed as something that is unique and of spiritual value - equality, economic justice, love, empathy, friendship, community, civic responsibility - they are all viewed as sacrilege to the God of Money, of absolute no worth, unless they can be turned into a commodities to be bought and sold and to be exploited for personal gain and profit, especially by you and me, because we have nothing else left to sell, except our souls.

So, Where Does this God Dwell?

Illustration #7

The Federal Reserve and the Temple of Human Sacrifice

On Constitutional Avenue and 20th Street in Washington, DC stands the Eccle Building, home of the Federal Reserve System. The granite four-story building is an austere building stripped of all nonessentials with massive iron doors, and the official Federal Reserve System web site describes the duties of the Federal Reserve as:

1. Oversee the federal reserve system
2. Conduct monetary policy
3. Provide financial system stability
4. Supervise and regulate financial institutions and activities
5. Foster payment and settlement system safety and efficiency

This sounds well and good, but beyond the façade and the massive iron doors of the temple dwells the God of Money cloaked in mystery and secrecy, for it is here at the Federal Reserve that we find the heart of the vampire system. It is here at the Temple of the God of Money that the priests of the temple determine the flow of our blood through the system – how much, at what price, and to whom. This priesthood of banking is organized into three branches, the Federal Reserve Board, the Regional Federal Reserve Banks, and the Federal Open Market Committee.

At the top of the Federal Reserve System are the seven governors of the Federal Reserve Board who are headquartered in Washington at the Eccles Building. They are appointed by the President of the United States with approval of the Senate to staggered fourteen-year terms of office to make it exceedingly difficult for the President to dominate the Board with his own appointees.

The seven governors share their power with the presidents of the twelve regional Reserve banks that serve the commercial banks in their region. The regional presidents of the Reserve are not appointed in Washington. They are elected by each regional board of directors for that regional bank. Six of the nine members of each board of directors are elected directly by the members of the commercial private banks, and three of the members of the board of directors are appointed by the Federal Reserve Board of Directors in Washington.

The third branch of the Federal Reserve System is the Federal Open Market Committee. The Open Market Committee is a hybrid of the Federal Reserve Board and the Regional Reserve Banks. The governors of the Federal Reserve Board have seven votes and the regional presidents of the Regional Reserve banking system have five votes. The regional representatives are rotated annually so that all the regional banks will be represented. The one exception is the New York City Regional Bank in the heart of Wall Street that has a permanent seat.

So how does our blood, our lives, our hopes, and our workflow through the heart of the system? There are two major control valves for the blood to flow through the body politic. One way is the Discount Window at each of the twelve Federal Reserve Regional Banks where commercial and depository institutions day to day borrow hundreds of million and even billions of dollars a day to make up for temporary shortages in their reserve requirements. Essentially, the Discount Window determines the interest rate at which the regional banks will loan to commercial bank and depository institutions which in turn will determine mortgage interest rates, credit card interest rates, and interest rates on personal and business loans etc. The regional banks in coordination with the Federal Reserve Board in Washington determine the rate at the Discount Window and depending on the rate they charge, the Federal Reserve can encourage of discourage borrowing and the flow of money to the private sector and at what cost.

The second way that the Fed controls the flow of money is the Open Market Window where the Fed buys and sells from $500 million dollars to several billion dollars of government securities a day on the open market. It is here in coordination with the Discount Window that the Fed can determine how much blood will flow through the government into the body politic. It is at the Open Market Window where the important decisions about the economy are made, and it is here that the priests of the temple cloak the truth in secrecy and mystery.

The Federal Open Market Committee meets to deliberate on the money supply eight to ten times a year, but the decisions are made in secret. Only six to ten weeks after the decisions are made is a brief report presented. The internal reports and memos and the economic analysis that supports the decisions made by the Committee are keep confidential for five years and the full transcript of the meetings are never released.

> As William Grieder noted in his book *Secrets of the Temple*, "No other agency of government, not even the CIA enjoys such privacy." He also cited a quote from Henry Ford Sr. on the mystery of the Federal Reserve where Henry Ford Sr. says, "It is well enough that the people of the nation do not understand our banking and monetary system for, if they did, I believe there would be a revolution tomorrow morning." (Grieder 55)

This is true. Behind the vault like temple doors, the priests of the God of Money perform blood sacrifices of such a magnitude that when the veil of illusion, secrecy, and mystery are swept away, and we understand what is happening to us, we will have no choice but to fight back. The bloody truth is quite simple. The prime reason that the Federal Reserve exists in its present form is to protect the value of money for the wealthiest classes in America. Essentially, we are talking about the vampire capitalists who make money off money, and at the top of this list of clients for the Federal Reserve are the bond holders who own America's debt. They are a very select group evidenced by the fact that the top 10% of the American families own 72% of the corporate and federal bonds and 86% of the state and local bonds. (Grieder 372)

> To put it another way, they own America. They are the loaners not the borrowers, the creditors not the debtors; they are the wealthy individuals, banks, and financial institutions that make money off interest. It is this group that the priests of the temple serve, and to illustrate the extent to which the Fed will go to protect this group, we will look at how America was slaughtered during the Reagan Era.

The Reagan Era & Trickle-Down Blood

In the 1980s, in response to a decade of double-digit inflation and Ronald Reagan's policies of tax reduction and deficit spending, the Fed cut the flow of money and raised interest rates. For example, twenty-year government bonds averaged only .6% when inflation was soaring in 1979 (well below the historical expectations of a fair return of 2% or less).

> In contrast, After the Fed implemented its hard money policies and raised interest rates, the real rate of long-term bonds jumped

> to 5.1%, roughly double the historical return. (Grieder 404) In addition, starting in 1997 when the Fed began to push up interest rates, commercial banking entered the most profitable era since World War II. Banker's net operating income increased 10.3% in 1980, grew another 9% in 1981 while large sectors of the economy were being destroyed and liquidated. (Grieder 411)
>
> Essentially, the blood was flowing upward to the Fed's true clients, the financial sector. In comparison Profession Gerald Epstein, an economist at the New School of Social Research, calculated that the before-tax-profits of the corporate sector, excluding finance, declined to an average 10.7% for the recession years of 1979 -1982 compared to the long term average of 15.9% profit for the years 1960 -1978. Commercial banks on the other hand, during the same period increased their average return on equity to 13.2% up from the long-term average of 10.4% (Grieder 412)

The businesses and industries most affected by the increase in interest rates were those that relied heavily on being able to borrow money on a routine bases, i.e. the auto industry, the oil business, the consumer credit industry, agrobusiness, the building and housing industry, and real estate etc. Also affected by the increase in interest rates and the resultant deflation of the economy and the hardening of the value of the dollar were businesses that depend on exporting its product and services, and companies sensitive to competition from abroad. Essentially, hard currency affected the international exchange market and made exports more expensive and imports cheaper. Agrobusiness exports were severely affected as were other exported. Imports nearly gutted the auto industry and the steel industry. Essential the American economy was sacrificed to the God of Money, and the priests of temple ripped the heart out of the body politic and ate it raw while it was still beating. Stocks were liquidated, farms were liquidated, real estate was liquidated, and whole industries were liquidated in the bloodletting.

Illustration #8

As for American labor, at the peak of the recession in December 1982, twelve million people were out of work, whereas, only 4.4 million of those out of work were drawing unemployment and a group just as large were working only part-time. In all, the dislocation totaled as many as 20 million American workers.(Grieder 455) Dr. M. Harvey Brenner of John Hopkins University calculated that 45,900 people died prematurely due to the swollen unemployment of 1974 -1975, casualties in a liquidation process that was less severe than the one that occurred in 1982. (Grieder 458)

The priests of the temple argue like the physicians in the middle ages who used blood suckers to purge their patient of their own blood. They argued that bloodletting is healthy for the body, and they call it "creative destruction," and when the vampire capitalist want to really be creative - they let the monster that dwells deep within their vaults free to roam beyond the temple doors, and they call it – war. War is the ultimate bloodletting for the vampire class because everyone, on both sides of the war, must borrow massive amounts of money to wage the war, and everyone must pay, winners and losers alike. Millions upon millions of lives are sacrificed, billion and billions of dollars are wasted and spilled on the battlefield, but that is not the end, after they have reduced whole countries to ruin, they make more money reconstructing what they destroyed.

Hiroshima Then and Now

Illustration # 9

The New Deal and the Band-Aid That Didn't Work

During the Great Depression the New Deal implemented a socialist overlay to a predominately capitalist economy, and by doing so saved us from the vampire capitalists who had brought us to the brink of disaster, the same vampire capitalists who are now dismantling the New Deal and will lead us, this time, to an economic apocalypse. The right-wing neo-liberals like to argue that the New Deal did not save us from the Great Depression. World War Two did. However, a stronger argument could be made for the fact that the war saved capitalism. Without the war we may have realized that we had not gone far enough and that we should have eliminated the capitalism at the core of our economy. We would have realized that we should have replaced it with an economic system where money circulated through the body politic in a way that nourishes everyone.

The thesis also ignores the fact that it was this socialist government during the war that created the greatest industrial war machine in history, defeated Japan and Germany in a two front war, and after the war instituted the G.I. Bill that made it possible for the working class people who fought in America's war to buy a home, start a business, or go to college. It also created a social-economic safety net to ameliorate the excesses of capitalism and protect its citizens against unemployment, secure their well-being when they grew old, and opened higher education to all our children.

Central to the New Deal's reforms of capitalism and its implementation of a mixed economy was its attempt to create a balance between big business, big government, and big labor; and it was the unions empowered by the New Deal that forced big business to offer pensions, fair wages, safe working conditions, and health plans to their employees. Even if a company wasn't unionized, it was the unions that caused the employer to offer these benefits to keep the unions out. In the process, America experienced the most prosperous period in its history and created the largest middle class in the world.

The globalization of manufacturing, finance, and the labor markets has broken down the balance that the New Deal attempted to create between business, labor, and government, and now the giant corporations that we created and subsidies have become global Leviathans in the service of the vampire class, economic imperialism, and the New World Order.

Illustration #10

The Leviathans of the New World Order: The Monster Grows

We have turned institutions that were created to serve us into monstrous Leviathans. Two hundred large transnational corporations now tower above the United States and the global economy. Comparing the gross national product of nation states to the annual sales of corporations, 69 of the 100 largest economies in the world in 2015 were private corporations.

Amongst this group, Walmart is the largest company in history. They employees 1.6 million people worldwide, most of which can't speak English. In 2012 Walmart registered $444 billion dollars in sales which is $20 billion dollars more than the Gross Nation Product of Austria.

Each week Walmart serves over 200 million customers at more than 10,400 stores in 27 countries. China's exports to Walmart account for an 11% growth in the total United States' trade deficit.

The Walton family own 50% of Walmart's stock. The family includes Helen, the widow of the late Walmart founder Sam Walton, and their four children, Alice, Sam, Jim, and John. The Walton family is worth over $102.7 billion dollars. Their estimated income from dividends is $880 million dollars a year, or $75 million for each of the Walmart heirs. This year the Walton family will receive $3.2 billion dollars in Walmart Dividends. If they actually worked for their dividend checks, they would be paid $1.56 million dollars per hour. Meanwhile Walmart workers start at $9/hr. and are routinely denied full-time work. (Making Change at Walmart)

This is your modern American aristocratic family of inherited wealth and power who pass your life blood on from one generation to another, feeding off us even when we die, alive like Zombies but dead. However, the Walton family are not an anomaly in America.

1. Daphne Greenwood and Edward Wolf have estimated in the study, "Changes in Wealth in the United States 1962-1983" that 50-70% of the wealth of households under age 50 was inherited. (Greenwood 5)

2. Laurence Kotlikoff and Lawrence Summers in their study, "The Role of Intergenerational Transfers in Aggregate Capital Accumulation" estimated that as much as 80% of personal wealth came either from direct inheritance or the income on inherited wealth. (Kotlifoff 89)

3. A study published by United for a Fair Economy in 1997 titled "Born on Third Base" found that of the 400 on the 1997 Forbes list of the wealthiest individuals and families in the United States, 42% inherited their way onto the list, another 6% didn't quite inherit their way onto the list but inherited wealth in excess of $50 million dollars, and another 7% started life off with a measly million. (Collin 61)

Chart #8

As noted earlier in the book, 10% of the population own America, and the top 20% of the population own 80% of the wealth. The rest of us are workers, and on the job, we are property with no rights or freedoms. We are a human resource like coal or oil or electricity, a human appendage to the cancerous growth of global corporations that have transcended their masters like a Frankenstein monster. These aberrant mutations to the body politic and our economic system are immortal. They continue to live through the bylaws of their charters from one generation to another into the indefinite future. On the other hand, you and I are mere mortals who live and die, as they go on growing larger and larger. Yet, despite their size and the fact that they dwarf the average American citizen, they are by law in the United States designated as "legal persons" with all the rights and freedoms of you and me without any of the responsibilities.

> In the 1886 case of Santa Clara v Southern Pacific (118 US 394, 1886), Chief Justice Waite of the Supreme Court orally directed the lawyers that the 14th Amendment of equal protection under the law clause guaranteed constitutional protections to corporations in addition to national persons, and the oral argument should focus on other issues in the case. (Calvert 656) Bancroft Davis noted, in the hand notes to the opinion that Chef Justice Morrison Waite began oral arguments by stating, "The court does not wish to hear argument on the question whether the provisions in the 14th Amendment to the Constitution, which forbids a State to deny to any person within its jurisdiction the equal protection of the law, applies to corporations. We are all of the opinion that it does." (118 US 394, 1886)

While the headnote is not part of the Court's opinion and thus not precedent, two years later, in Pembina Consolidated Silver Mining Co v Pennsylvania -125 US 181, 1888, the Court clearly affirmed the doctrine holding, "Under the designation of 'person' there is no doubt that a private corporation is included in the 14th Amendment. Such corporations are merely associations of individuals united for a special purpose and permitted to do business under a particular name and have a succession of members without dissolution." Official Court Syllabus in the United States Report, (Calvert, 650).

> At this point in history the corporate Leviathans became legal persons with the rights of an individual person, just like us, but that is merely a mask to hide the monster behind a legal fiction. This 'person' is not human. It is inhuman, and it has a singular pursuit and only one objective, and that is to maximize profit at any cost. A corporation-as-a-person is incapable of feelings, and it is totally devoid of empathy and a sense of responsibility to others. Quite simply, in human terms, corporations, as 'persons', are certifiably insane psychopaths capable of mass murder and unspeakable crimes.

Even the crime of mass murder is irrelevant to this monster if the cost of committing the crime is less than the profit to be made being a murderer on a scale that would horrify us if a single person did it or even if a country did it in the act of war. For example, In a law suit in which a car slammed into the rear end of Patricia Anderson's car and caused the gas tank to explode, it was revealed that General Motors determined that the cost of correcting the flaw in the design of the vehicle in the following way: (1) They multiplying the 500 fuel-fed-fire fatalities occurring each year because of their faulty design by $200,000 dollars, the estimated cost to General Motors in legal damages for each potential wrongful death suit. (2) They then divided that figure by the 41 million cars that they estimated were on the road with that fatal design and determined that it would cost them $2.40/ fatality if they did nothing and just let people die. However, to redesign the cars and correct the flaw in the cars that were on the road, they estimated that it would cost them $8.59/car. This meant that the company saved $6.19/car if they simple allowed people to die year after year, or, in other worlds, it was cost efficient to commit mass murder.

GM is not an isolated case. Corporate crimes dwarf street crime. For example, the Federal Bureau of Investigation estimates that the cost yearly of burglaries and robberies in the United States amounted to $4.5 billion dollars in 2014, but just the savings and loan fraud of the 80s alone cost the American taxpayer an estimated $300-$500 billion dollars. Added to that is an estimated $40 billion dollars a year in repair fraud, $15 billion dollars a year in deceptive financial practices, and billions upon billions of dollars stolen and robbed in cheating depositors, overcharging customers, food contamination, adulterated medication, illegal marketing, failure to report safety defects, workplace hazards, sanitation violations, air pollution, ocean dumping, climate denial, price fixing, foreign bribery, and wage theft, but that is not the worst of their crimes.

> Corporations commit violent crimes against living human beings that reach a scale of horror compared to the horrors of war. For example, compared to the 14,000 Americans murdered every year in America as estimated by the FBI and the 58,220 Americans killed in the Vietnam War, it is estimated that 54,000 Americans die every year on the job or from occupational diseases, and tens of thousands of Americans fall victim every year to the silent violence of pollution, contaminated food, hazardous consumer products, and hospital malpractice. (Mokhiber)
>
> I repeat. These monsters, by charter, have only one imperative - to maximize profit. All other qualities that we define as human – love of family, a sense of community, national pride, civic responsibility, empathy for the suffering of others, common decency – they are all irrelevant and meaningless to the bottom line. In fact, if as the head of a corporation you were to express any of the above human qualities in a way that would undermine the prime imperative - maximizing profit, you could be sued by the stockholders for violating the corporate charter. This was the case of Henry Ford.

In the case of Dodge versus Ford Motor Company 170N.W.668 (Michigan 1919) the Michigan Supreme Court held that Henry Ford had to operate the Ford Motor Company in the interest of its shareholders. He could not operate it in any way that would benefit the employees and/or customers and/or community and nation-at-large at the expense of the shareholders unless he could demonstrate that it improved the bottom line. So, who are these stockholders? Eighty-four percent of all stocks owned by Americans belong to the wealthiest 10% of households and that includes everyone's stakes in pension plans, 401(K)'s, and individual retirement accounts, as well as trust funds, mutual funds, and college savings programs like 529 plans.

> The stockholders argue that they have a right to their shares in the profits because they risk their capital by investing in our corporations and their future. In fact, the only time that the so called "investors" in stocks actually invest in a company is at the initial offerings when the company goes public. It is only then that the money directly goes to the company. Statistically 1% of the money in the market goes to direct investment in initial offerings and 99% to speculation, but when you include in the equation the corporate buybacks that corporations institute so as to protect themselves from corporate raiders and hostile take-overs, the amount of money directly invested in corporations is less than 0% - which is to say more money is going out of the market than is going into it. Or as Marjorie Kelly wrote in *The Devine Right of Capital: Dethroning the Corporate Aristocracy* "Rather than capitalizing companies, the stock market has been decapitalizing them. Stockholders for decades have been an immense drain on corporations." (Kelly 35)

So, let's be clear, the stock market is not about investment. It is a game of casino economics, and for the most part, the stockholders are like the aristocrats of old that we fought against. They do nothing for their money. For the most part, they are passive absentee owners and largely an unproductive body of constantly changing speculators whose sole function is to feed off of the global corporate Leviathans whose sole purpose is to maximize profit and feed off of us. These Leviathans are not "persons." They are not like a normal healthy human being that has growth periods and periods of decline that are part of the cycle of life of death and rebirth. They do not seek stability and the harmony of its parts where blood as money nourishes all the parts, each and every cell, each and every one of us, for the well-being of the whole. These monsters were not created to serve the common good. They are a cancerous growth that is spreading throughout the globe.

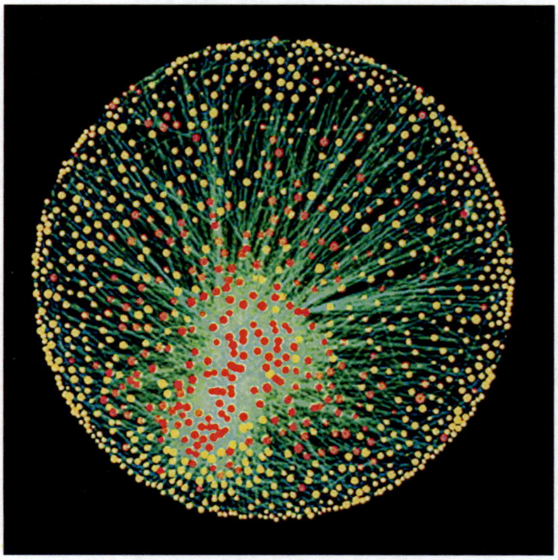

Chart #9

Global Reach

Global Reach: The Cancer Grows

The above illustration is from a study by theorists at the Swiss Federal Institute of Technology in Zurich. In the study of transnational companies world-wide, they identified 1318 (in yellow) corporations with interlocking ownership as the core network of global power. The 1318 corporations identified generated 20% of the global operating revenues, and they owned a majority of the shares in the world's largest blue chip and manufacturing firms, which accounts for additional 60% of the global revenues. The research group was able to further untangle the web of power and reduce it to 147 corporations (in red) that are so tightly networked together. They control 40 percent of the total wealth of the network. (Coghlan)

Over the past quarter century, the growth of global corporations has accelerated. In 1970 there were about 7000 parent transnational corporations, but, today, the study above done by the Swiss Federal Institute of Technology in Zurich approximates the number of transnationals to be more like 47,000. Approximately 90% of these transnationals are based in the industrial world, but they have 207,000 foreign subsidiaries world-wide. However, the large number of transnational global corporations can be misleading because it is calculated that the 300 largest global corporations own and/or control at least 1/4th of the world's total productive assets worth approximately $5 trillion US dollars, and as noted in the study done by the Swiss Federal Institute of Technology in Zurich, basically, "in effect, 1% of the companies were able to control 40 percent of the entire network of transnationals, and most of them were financial institutions." Or, in other words, the blood banks are at the heart of the New World Order, and they control the flow of blood throughout the world. (Coghlan)

The Blood Banks

1	**ICBC** (China)	**$ 2.95** trillion	18,000 outlets 108 branches globally
2	**HSBC Holdings** (UK)	**$ 2.68** trillion	6,600 offices 55 million customers
3	**Deutsche Bank** (Germany)	**$ 2.60** trillion	2,963 branches 46 million customers
4	**Crédit Agricole** (France)	**$ 2.58** trillion	60 countries 21 million clients
5	**BNP Paribas** (France)	**$ 2.51** trillion	
6	**Mitsubishi UFJ** (Japan)	**$ 2.49** trillion	
7	**Barclays PLC** (UK)	**$ 2.41** trillion	
8	**JPMorgan Chase** (US)	**$ 2.39** trillion	
9	**China Constr. B.** (China)	**$ 2.36** trillion	
10	**Japan Post Bank** (Japan)	**$ 2.12** trillion	

Chart #10

The Financial Institutions That Govern the New World Order

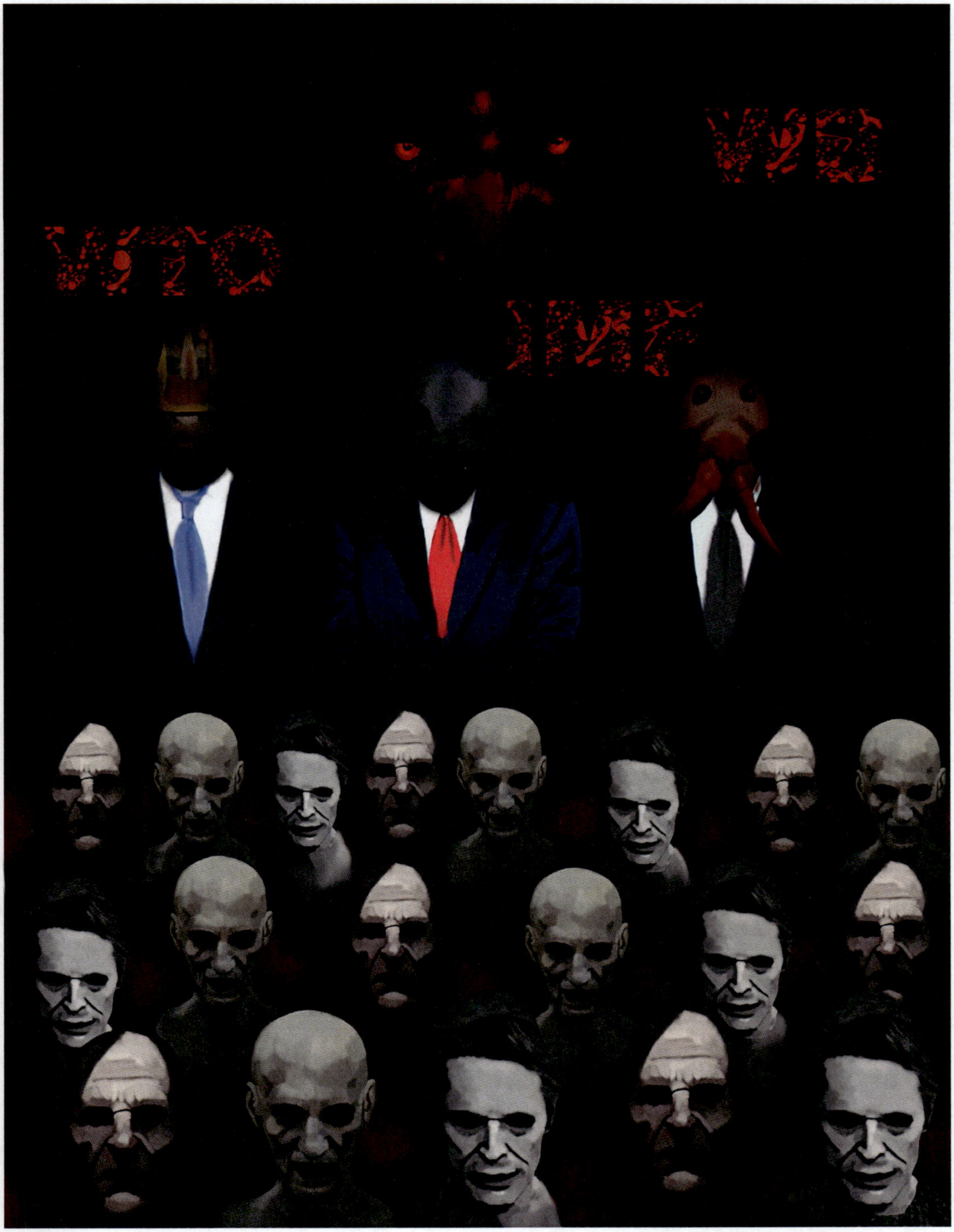

Illustration #11

The transnational banks and the global financial institutions that are emerging are at the core of the New World Order of vampire capitalism, and if the vampire capitalist have their way, through the banking and financial institutions and the Leviathans they have created, they will control the flow of blood throughout the world and transform nation-states into corporate states, feudal fortresses to protect the new global aristocracy of wealth and money.

In the New World Order, there are three major global financial institutions that have become global economic governing institutions that transcend the nation-state and are usurping their power. These three global institutions play a major role in controlling the flow of our life blood globally. They are the International Monetary Fund, the World Bank, and the World Trade Organization. They are non-democratic institutions dominated by major banking, corporate, and financial interests from around the world. The same vampires that are sucking us dry at home are taking our blood, our hopes and dreams, and exporting them as investments and loans to new host nations. The host nations are usually underdeveloped countries dominated by its own elite class of vampire capitalist who are usually not hindered as we are in the United States by the shredded remnants of a representative government, and they can rule by absolute terror and fear. These domestic vampires can usually ensure that there will be no laws, regulations, taxes, or labor unions to hinder their bottom-line appetites, and there will be an unlimited supply of cheap and child labor to feed off.

The World Bank, International Monetary Fund, and the World Trade Organization came out of the Bretton Wood Conference in 1944, and their original intent was to stabilize the world economy in opposition to the economic chaos that existed prior to the Second World War, an economic chaos that was believed to be one of the major causes of the war. That was then, but this is now, and even though institutions like this could still serve the common good if they were truly representative of the people, they are not.

International Monetary Fund

Originally, the stated goal of the International Monetary Fund was to stabilize currency rates and balance of payment deficits, or in other words, prevent more blood from going out of the nation than was coming in. However, over time, as the IMF has embraced the free market neo-liberal ideology of the vampire capitalists, the terms for loaning money to desperate underdeveloped and less developed countries have become more and more oppressive. Rather than the conditions and terms of repayment benefiting the debtor country and the global economic community as a whole, the terms of repayment exposed the veins of the debtor nation to the vampire capitalists who then bleed the host nation, especially the poor.

For example, as a condition for obtaining a loan, (1) the IMF requires the reduction of tariffs so as to open up the domestic market to an increased influx of foreign products and services thereby undermining the efforts of the host nation to create domestic alternatives and diversify its industrial and economic capacities. (2) The IMF demands an increase in interest rates to cool the economy and reduce inflation to protect the value of the money owed. This discourages domestic investment and borrowing, and the only winners are the financial institutions and banks that get to charge the increased interest rates. (3) The IMF also pushes for the privatization of government assets that insiders then can purchase at bargain basement prices, and, at the same time, they demand cutbacks in government services and programs, programs and services that reduce poverty, improve health care, and support education.

Basically, the supposed intent of the International Monetary Fund was to repair an economic system that was losing more blood than it was taking in, but, in fact, the IMF turns the leaks in the economy into puncture holes.

The World Bank

Like the International Monetary Fund, the World Bank was originally well intended. Established along with the IMF at Bretton Wood in 1944, it established five financial institutions, two of which we will focus on here as most relevant of the five in tracking where the blood goes. They are the International Bank for Reconstruction and Development and the International Development Association. The IBRD makes development loans, guarantees loans, and offers analytical and advisory services. It borrows at low interest rates by selling bonds in private capital markets in First World countries, and it then makes near-market interest loans to 'credit worthy countries' in the Third World and elsewhere. It has made about $360 billion in loans over its lifetime and currently loans $10.5 billion a year for some ninety new operations in thirty-six countries. (World Bank) The International Development Association gives loans to countries that are 'usually not credit worthy' in international financial markets. IDA loans carry no interest, but a 0.75 percent administrative charge is paid every year. The IDA, averaging $6 million a year in lending to the poorest countries, is funded from member governments' national budget. (World Bank)

Like the International Monetary Fund, the World Bank in 1944 was established with good intent. The original purpose of the World Bank was to facilitate investment of capital for productive purposes in less developed countries by infusing the endemic countries with more blood to increase productivity and the health and prosperity of the country. They planned to accomplish this goal by promoting, coordinating, and participating in loans with private investors. This sounds all well and good, but, once again, that was then and this is now, and if you tear away the mask of respectability and pseudo economic science that the priesthood of the temple have embraced, we see, as with the International Monetary Fund, that the World Bank imposes the same predatory economic structural adjustments and conditions for obtaining a loan and rescheduling and refinancing loans in arrears. Even when they do finance a public project, it often turned out to be just another way for the domestic vampires can get in on the feast. They do this by causing the government that they dominate and control to take out loans for public projects that end up as sweetheart deals for themselves and the transnationals that they partner with. To compound the evil, in many instances, the projects are never finished or their value to the community is questionable and often disastrous for the people of the country because they are left with the debt that has to be paid with their blood.

For example, in Kenya, the World Bank has invested some $29 million in the Bura irrigation scheme. But when President of Kenya, Daniel Arap Moi, inspected the site, he found "eroded irrigation canals, abandoned plots, poor crops, tumbledown and unsanitary housing, zebra grazing on irrigated land, and an air of general desolation and decay."(Gunnell 18) According to Gunnell "a confidential World Bank mid-term evaluation report at the beginning of 1985 reported that Bura's tenants, aside from being so disaffected that a fifth of them had deserted their plots, suffered mortality and morbidity rate several times higher than the national average." Even though the project had invested almost $50,000 per family to be benefited, the bank report found severe malnutrition widespread among the beneficiaries. Correspondent Barbara Gunnell concluded, "The real loser is the Kenyan government, or as President Moi pointed out, future generations of Kenyans who will go on paying World Bank interest on the loan. Loan repayments will be just as high as if the World Bank's economic appraisal that the scheme could expect a 13 percent rate of return had been correct." (Gunnell 18).

The bottom line is, rather than the conditions and terms of repayment benefiting the debtor country and the global economic community as a whole, the terms of repayment exposed the veins of the debtor nation to the vampire capitalists who extract payment at the expense of the host nation leaving it poorer than it was when it reached out for a helping hand. Even the World Bank's own experts know this, but they are afraid to look in the mirror and see the blood on their lips. For example, the Structural Adjustment Participatory Review (SAPRI) was created by the World Bank and a network of 250 Non-Government Organizations to improve the understanding about the impact of the loan and adjustment policies implemented by the World Bank and the international banking and private financial institutions that worked in cooperation with the World Bank. The group concluded that "Many of the predicted gains in efficiency, competition, savings, and revenue from privatization and the implementing of neoliberal economic policies have failed to materialize, quite simply, everything that the International Monetary Fund and the World Bank has done, in terms of structural adjustment and in terms of conditions for obtaining a loan, has been a total failure." (Peet p 161-162).

World Trade Organization

The World Trade Organization was founded in 1995. Its stated purpose was to insure open and equal market access and nondiscrimination in the trade of products, services, ideas, and capital. Like the International Monetary Fund and the World Bank, the WTO masks its real intent behind high sounding words, and it would have us believe that they serve the common good, but the International Trade Organization, like the International Monetary Fund and the World Bank, does not represent the people or the common wealth. It does not represent the American people, or the host nation, or the global community at large. Like the International Monetary Fund and the World Bank it is a nondemocratic institution that makes important decisions about international trade and domestic policies out of the public view and in secret. "It has no written-by-laws, makes decisions by consensus. It has never taken a vote on anything. It holds no public hearings and has never opened its processes to public view. Its meeting rooms do not even have a section for the public to observe its activities, and the court-like-rulings on trade are not made by United States style due process." (Wachtel 37)

What is most horrifying about the World Trade Organization is that it has become a nondemocratic global economic governing body. It has judicial and enforcement powers far beyond any other international institution including the United Nations, and it represents, as the protestors in Seattle claimed in a press statement in 1999, the greatest transfer of political and economic power from a nation-states to a global institution in history. The WTO has the power to rule on a nation's right to pass legislation, enforce regulations and environmental standards, and implement economic governmental policies that WTO adjudicates as standing in the way of free trade. What is defined as "free trade" is decided on by the WTO tribunals that have the power to impose severe sanctions on the offending state, and these sanctions are enforced by over 153 nations that are members of the WTO, and they represent 100% of the world trade. Quite simply, the WTO is not about democracy. It is about controlling and regulating democracy, and despite what many people would like to believe, when we are talking about the reality of "globalism" in the capitalist world that exists today, we are not talking about a world where we all come together to work for the common good. We are not talking about reaching across borders of language, race, and class conflict. We are not talking about ridding the world of ethnic cleansing, the wars of nations, religions, and all the other forms of "isms" and identity politics that create walls of meaningless babel between us, nor are we talking about ridding the world of poverty and starvation. We are talking about Vampire Capitalism on a global scale, and its goal is to create open borders so that it can feast on each and every one of us world-wide. We are talking about a cancerous growth that must be stopped because it can't stop itself. Having said this, we have now come to the final depths of the Capitalist Hell and the final truth.

Capitalism must continually grow, or it will die.

Learn or Die

Capitalism must grow and continually find new investments to absorb capital and pay off the compound interest that is at the core of the need for more. This need for continuous growth is estimated to be 3%, a figure that reflects the prime interest rate on average for a healthy investment and banking system to sustain profit and continually loan out money. This is the engine of capitalism, and it is what makes it a dooms-day-machine. Like the monster machines in the movie *The War of the Worlds* that gobble up human beings and use their blood for fertilizer, the corporate Leviathans in the real story hidden behind the science fiction horror are not aliens from without. They are the aliens from within that are spreading the cancerous growth of run-away-capitalism throughtout the world at an accelerated rate.

In 1820 (based on 1990 dollars) Agnus Maddison calculated that the total output of goods and services in the capitalist world economy was worth $694 billion dollars. By 1913 it had raised to $2.7 trillion dollars, and by 1950, it reached $5.3 trillion dollars. In 1973 it stood at $16 trillion, by 2003 it was $41 trillion dollars, and by 2009 it was at $56.2 trillion dollars and rising. (Harvey 26) Globalization has accelerated this growth and the depletion of our natural resources and the pollution of our air, water, and soil. Forests are shrinking, water tables are falling, vast expanses of soil are eroding, wetlands are disappearing, fisheries are collapsing, range lands are deteriorating, rivers are running dry, coral reefs are dying, plant and animal species are disappearing, temperatures are rising, global climate change is accelerating, and the world's population keeps growing to keep up with capitalism's need for more consumers. An ecologist, John Terborgh, after a trip to a small African country, described the acceleration of resource depletion in the global era.

> "Everywhere I went, foreign commercial interests were exploiting resources after signing contracts with the autocratic government. Prodigious logs, four and five feet in diameter, were coming out of the forests, oil and natural gas were being exported from the coastal region, offshore fishing rights had been sold to foreign interests, and exploration for oil and minerals were under way in the interior. The exploitation of resources

in North America during the five-hundred-year post-discovery era followed a typical sequence –fish, furs, game, timber, farming virgin soil – but because of the hugely expanded scale of today's economy and the availability of myriad sophisticated technologies, exploitation of all the resources in poor developing countries now goes on at the same time. In a few years, the resources of this African country and others like it will be sucked dry." (Terborgh)

Harbingers of Doom

Twenty-five years ago, The Union of Concerned Scientists and more than 1700 independent scientists including most living Nobel laureates in the sciences, penned the 1992 "World Scientists' Warning to Humanity." It was a call to end environmental destruction, and it warned that "a great change in our stewardship of the Earth and the life on it is required, if vast human misery is to be avoided." On the twenty-fifth anniversary of their call for change, 15,364 scientists from 184 countries have looked back to that period compared to today, and they see that the problems that they saw then have gotten much worse. Here are some of the alarming changes which have taken place in the last 25 years.

1. The amount of fresh water available per head of population worldwide will be reduced by 26%.
2. The number of oceans "dead zones" - places where little can live because of pollution and oxygen starvation – will increased by 75%.
3. Nearly 300 million acres of forest will be lost, mostly to make way for agricultural land.
4. Global carbon emissions and average temperatures will show continued significant increases.
5. Human population will rise by 35%.
6. Collectively the number of mammals, reptiles, amphibians, birds, and fish in the world will fall by 29%. (Ripple 1026-1028)

They're Devouring Our Planet

The Economics of Ecosystems and Biodiversity is a global institution based in Geneva, Switzerland at the International Environment House and is hosted by the United Nations Environment Program. The TEEB's mission is to analyze and measure global problems of biodiversity loss and ecosystem degradation in terms of economic and human welfare. The following chart projects into the future our path of self-destruction and the devouring of our planet.

Illustration #12

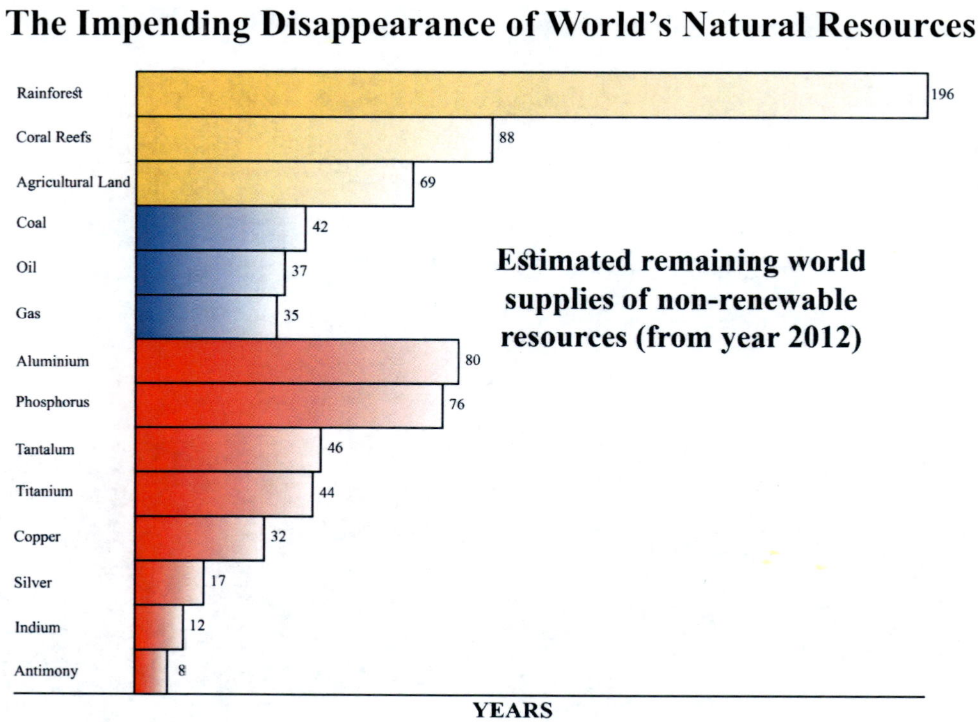

Chart #11

According to the above chart it is estimated that,

1. By 2030 the Artic will be ice-free in the summer.
2. By 2050 a third of the land plants and animal species will be extinct due to climate change.
3. In 75 years, the Indonesian Rainforest will be gone.
4. In 196 years, the Brazilian Rainforest will be gone.
5. In the next 35-42 years gas, oil, and coal will be gone.
6. In the next 7-45 years key rare earth minerals will be gone.

And, finally, in 2060 the dangerous 2 degree C warming threshold will likely be reached. Carbon concentrations have not been this high since the Pliocene period between 3 million and 5 million years ago when global average temperatures were 3 degrees or 4 degrees Centigrade hotter than today. During that period, the Artic was ice-free, sea levels were about 40 meters higher, jungles covered northern Canada, and Florida was under water along with coastal locations we now call New York City, London, Shanghai, Hong Kong, Sydney and many others.

The End of the Journey

Illustration #13

Illustration #14

What are we looking at here? Is this the end of the journey for a society that has nurtured vampire capitalism and glorifies narcissism, a society where we all pursue our own individual greed, where we take more than we give, and we ignore the consequences of our acts? Is this a society where deep in the darkness of our collective unconscious this monstrous reality has grown? What is it that we are looking at? Has the vampire capitalist created something far more evil than they could ever imagine, something that now has a life of its own? Is this what we mean by the Devil, or is it Devine Justice, or both? Whatever it is, the lesson is clear. Capitalism must grow or it will die, and if it continues to grow, it will kill us all, capitalist and worker alike. This we must learn, or we will die.

Capitalism will kill us all!

Throughout the world and in the United States neo-liberalism and vampire capitalism have generated an overwhelming feeling of despair, a feeling that it is hopeless to resist the so called "New World Order" of global capitalism. Voting seems a waste of time in the one-dollar-one-vote pseudo-democracy. Labor unions seem to be ineffective against the power of the global Leviathans that dominate the world's economy. We fear layoffs, downsizing, the relocation of our jobs abroad, and we see the homeless on the street and say to ourselves, "That could be me. I'm one paycheck away."

We live in a parasitic economy that is a royal feast for some, a constant struggle for survival for most, and a living hell for many of us. Though we are capable of producing an abundance of wealth that will improve the quality of life for everyone, the vampire capitalists search the world for cheap slave and child labor to maximize their profit and to feed their blood lust, and now, they are spreading this disease throughout the world, endangering the survival of the human race and the life of the planet itself.

In principle, socialism should be able to take advantage of the increasing awareness that capitalism is failing us, and it is an evil that feeds off our very life blood. But, tragically, just at the moment when capitalism has revealed its fatal flaws and the horrors of its true nature, socialism, as it exists today, has revealed its own weaknesses as an alternative. For example, the Soviet Union in its collapse revealed the fatal flaws of a nondemocratic command economy.

Western Europe and the America of the New Deal have also failed to fully realize all their hopes and dreams of a new future, primarily because they have retained capitalism as the core to their economy, and, therefore, at their best have only been able to ameliorate capitalism's worse effects and provide a minimal safety net for its victims.

> To save ourselves from the evil of vampire capitalism and the apocalypse of self-destruction that will come if we continue to allow the spread of this cancer, we need a new vision of our future, new political and economic paradigms to guide us back to a future of new hopes and dreams. This should be relatively easy for us to do because the answers have always been with us. They are rooted in our finest traditions and lie deep in the ethical and moral roots of the American dream.

Unfortunately, for so many years, we have spent most of our time creating a labyrinth of lies and self-delusion, and we have become madder and madder as we face one dead end after another. It seems to me that this is what the myth of the Minotaur and the Labyrinth is all about. The Minotaur is the truth that gores us because we do not have the courage to face the truth. The truth is that our future is dead in the womb if we continue on this path, and we don't find our way out of this labyrinth of illusions and lies.

Fortunately, the truth is far more straight-forward and liberating than the lies that we tell ourselves. For example, "We hold these truths to be self-evident, that all men are created equal, that they are endowed by their Creator with certain unalienable Rights that among these are Life, Liberty, and the pursuit of Happiness." Or "that the nation, shall have a new birth of freedom, and that government of the people, by the people, for the people, shall not perish from the earth." Simple words, straight forward and profound, and they rocked our universe and caused us to dream great dreams, but now they are like ghosts to us, ghosts of a dream that never came true because democracy is a revolution that has never been won. I repeat.

Democracy is a revolution that has never been won.

PART TWO: The Myth of Democracy

Voter Rights and the Myth of Democracy

Democracy is a revolution that has never been won. From its very inception the United States was not a democratic country. Few Americans had the right to vote. Voting was restricted to male property owners, and the only national office that male property owners had the right to vote for in the original Constitution was the House of Representatives. It was not until 1913 and the passing of the 17th Amendment to the Constitution that senators were directly elected by the American people for a 6 year term of office, but even then, the election of senators was and is staggered so that only 1/3rd of the senators comes up for election every 2 years. This, along with the staggering of the terms office for the members of House of Representatives (2 years), the Presidency of the United States (4 years), and the Senate (as noted 6 years); conspire to thwart a simple majority and the will of the people at any given time.

As for the Presidency, to this day, in fact, the people do not elect the President of the United States. Nor does he or she necessarily reflect the vote of the majority of the American people. The President of the United States is chosen by electors under a constitutional grant of authority delegated to the legislatures of each state. This is to say that after the American people have voted in the November election for the president, it is not until the middle of December when the president is actually elected by the Electoral College consisting of 528 electors with each state determining the manner by which its state electors are chosen. Each state has as many electors as they have members in the House of Representatives and in the Senate, and it takes an absolute majority of all the 528 electors nation-wide to win the presidency.

There are two important points to be made about the Electoral College and how it does not truly represent the will of the people, and it is a non-democratic institution that is a danger to democracy. One, the electors are "pledged" to vote as the people voted in the presidential election, but they are not required to by law. This was apparent in the 2000 presidential election between Al Gore and George W. Bush. The election was close, and it came down to who won the swing state of Florida, but a significant number of votes in that state were in question because of what many believed was a faulty and corrupted ballot. The Supreme Court of the United States stopped a recount that had been ordered by the Supreme Court of Florida. That decision gave Bush the electoral college votes for that state and secured Bush a victory in the presidential election over Gore even though Gore won the popular vote nation-wide. The point here is that while the vote in Florida was being contested in the courts, the State Legislature of Florida that was dominated by Republicans threatened that, if the court adjudicated against Bush in favor of Gore, they would recall all their electoral college delegates and put up a new slate of electors that would be directed to vote for Bush, regardless of the popular vote. What this should tell you is that we only have the right to elect the President of the United States at the pleasure of our betters, and whenever it pleases them, they can take that illusion away from us.

Winner-Take-All and Swing States

The Bush versus Gore election highlighted another serious flaw in the Electoral College System of voting for the President of the United State and how this system of voting undermines a system of democracy where every American's vote counts. The critical flaw I am referring to is that the Electoral College System is a winner-take-all system of voting state-by-state, meaning that if the candidate wins the majority of the votes in the state, the candidate wins all the electoral college votes in that state. This winner-take-all system makes it possible for a candidate to win the majority of the votes in America and lose the election. This was the case in the Gore versus Bush and Hillary Clinton versus Donald Trump. In both instances the loser won the popular vote, but in the winner-take-all electoral college system, they lost the election.

This system also means that candidates in the winner-take-all system do not have to focus on sure-thing-state because in those states the loser's votes don't count. Elections, therefore, focus on what are called "swing state," states that are uncertain. This often means that an election is determined by only five or six states that are up for grabs, resulting in the following picture of the United States according to voting power.

The UNITED *SWING* STATES of AMERICA

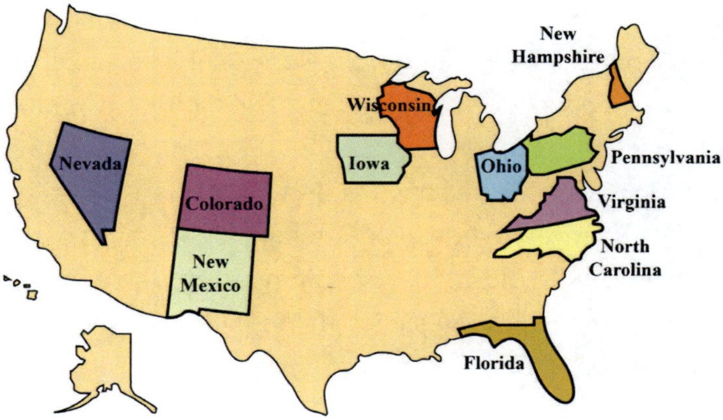

Chart #12

History of Voting Rights and the Fight for Universal Suffrage

As for the restriction in the original Constitution of the United States of voting to only male citizen who owned property, the reasoning behind this restriction was expressed by John Adam, one of the shapers of the Declaration of Independence and the Constitution, when he said,

> "The same reasons which will induce you to admit all men who have no property to vote with those who have...will prove that you ought to admit women and children, for generally speaking women and children have as good judgement and as independent minds as those men who are wholly destitute of property, these last being to all intents and purposes as much dependent on others who will please to feed, clothe, and employ them as women are upon their husbands or children on their parents...Depend upon it, sir, it is dangerous to open so fruitful a source of controversy and altercation as would be opened by attempting to alter the qualifications of voters; there will be no end to it. New claims will arise; women will demand to vote, lads from twelve to twenty-one will think their rights not enough attended to; and every man who has not a farthing, will demand an equal voice with any other, in all acts of state. It tends to confound and destroy all distinctions and prostates all ranks to one common level." - John Adams in a letter to John Sullivan 1776 (Keyssar 1)

Even among males, the property restriction was prohibitive. For example, a study of New York State before 1820 indicated that 2/3rd of the adult males were unable to meet the property requirement in order to vote for members of the United States Senate and 1/3rd were unable to meet the much lower property requirements for voting for the legislature. Eliminating the property requirement in New York State tripled the electorate for the senatorial races and increased the number of male voters qualified to vote by 50% for the Assembly. Even then, however, attempts to restrict voter rights by other means intensified with the flood of immigration, the transformation of the United States from an agrarian society to an industrial society, and the growth of a large urban population.

The exclusion from the right to vote continued in large part for African Americans, Native Americans, women of all races, immigrants, the working poor, and citizens on relief. The property requirement was replaced by states throughout the United States by poll taxes, literacy tests, prohibitive registration and residence requirements, grandfather clauses, and laws that withheld the right to vote for naturalized citizens for extended periods of time after becoming citizens.

Quite simply, in the 1800s and early 1900s the vast majority of the American people, East and West, North, and South did not have the right to vote in a country that was dedicated at its inception to be a government for, by, and of the people. It wasn't until 1920 when women, who represented half the population, won the right to vote, but this was only after a prolonged and massive effort. The following passage from Alexander Kyssar's study, *The Right to Vote: The Contested History of Democracy in the United States* is very descriptive of that struggle.

> "To get the world "male" in effect out of the Constitution cost the women of the country fifty-two years of pause less campaign… During that time they were forced to conduct 56 campaigns of referendum to male voters, 480 campaigns to get legislatures to submit suffrage amendments to voters, 47 campaigns to get state constitutional conventions to write woman suffrage into state constitutions, 277 campaigns to get state party conventions to include woman suffrage planks, 30 campaigns to get

> presidential and 19 campaigns with 19 successive party conventions to adopt woman suffrage planks in party platforms and 19 campaigns with 19 successive Congresses" – Carrie Chapman Catt and Nettie R. Shuler, Woman Suffrage and Politics (1926) (Keyssar 172)

Even with the passing of the 19th Amendment that gave women the right to vote, the restrictions on voting based on race, class, immigration status, and ethnic background were still in place and effected women as well as men. It wasn't until the 1960s that we experienced another major victory for universal suffrage, and that came with the inspired civil rights movement that courageously pursued social, economic and political equality in the face of violent opposition highlighted nationally by the shooting of James Meredith as he walked from Tennessee to Mississippi in what was called The March On Fear; the bombing of the 16th Street Baptist Church where four little girls, Addie Mae Collins (14 years old) Cynthia Wesley (14), Carole Robertson (14), and Carol Denise McNair (11) died; the murder of three civil rights workers in Mississippi during Freedom Summer; and the assassination of Martin Luther King that ignited the riots in Watt and race riots throughout the country.

Out of this turmoil and struggle came a series of voter rights acts and amendments that finally put an end to the major obstacles to voting right for African Americans in the United States. By 1975, the nation had witnessed a far-reaching legal revolution. What occurred in the swipe of a decade was not only the re-enfranchisement of African Americans but the abolition of nearly all remaining limits on the right to vote, i.e. poll taxes, literacy tests, pauper exclusions, and good character exclusions had all been abolished. Property and tax requirements for voting in special elections were eliminate, residency qualifications were drastically broadened, the voting age was lowered to 18 years old, and language barriers were dropped.

For the first time in our history, after years of struggle and blood shed, after proving our worth as citizens by fighting and dying and working for our country, we had finally achieved universal suffrage only to see that it was an illusion, a farce, and that America is not a country of one-man-one-vote. It was a country of one-dollar-one-vote.

Illustration #15

One Dollar - One Vote

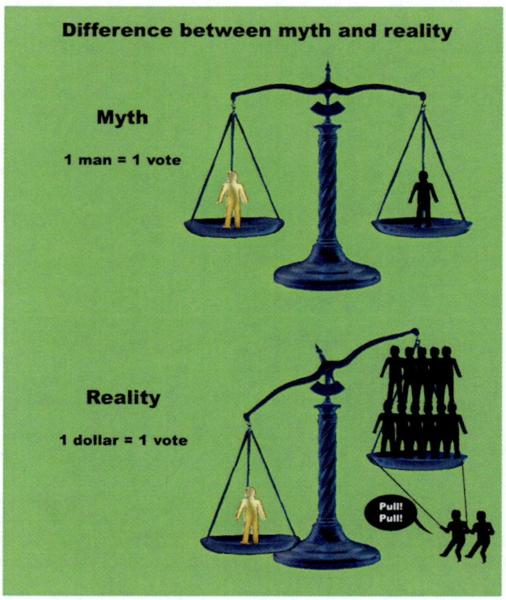

Chart #13

Money in Politics: One-Dollar-One-Vote

Money has always been a part of American politics, but today with the Supreme Court decision in Citizen United and Speechnow.org versus FEC, the doors have been flung open for unlimited amounts of blood money to pour into political campaigns, lobbying, foundations, think tanks, PACs and Super PACs to buy elections, formulate public policy, influence legislation, and rationalize greed.

In the one-dollar-one-vote system of politics in the United States, candidates for office campaign for years before the next election, and most of their time is spent on fund raising. It is estimated that members of Congress spend 30% to 70% of their time in office fund raising for the next election. (Long, Will) They do this for good reason. For example, according to the Center for Responsive Politics, during the 2012 election cycle the candidates running for a Senate seat who spent the most money won 79% of the time, and the candidates running for the House of Representatives who spent the most money won 94% of the time. (Hahn, Jonah)

It was reported by the Washington Post that according to the campaign finance watchdog opensecrets.org that 2.4 billion dollars was spent on the presidential election and 4 billion dollars was spent on the congressional races. With that much money, it was noted, that you could fund the Corporation for Public Broadcasting for 15 years without any reliance on corporate funding, fix the Flint, Michigan lead pipe problem 30 times over or give every public school teacher in the country a $2000 dollar raise. (Ingraham)

Where does the money come from? Most of the money comes from those who donate $2500 dollars or more, or 0.05 percent of the citizens of the United States. This means that 99.95% of the American population are not a part of the America For Sale campaign where all the important issues are bought up before they even vote. The buyers, for the most part, are corporations and the very wealthy. For example, according to followmymoney.org a not-for-profit dedicated to following the money in politics, in the last 5 years, the top 200 most politically active corporations in America spent $5.8 billion dollars on lobbying and political campaigns, and much of this money is dark money, meaning that like gangsters, corporations and the super-rich launder their money by channeling it through dummy non-profit fronts so that when the money comes out the other end into the hands of the politicians or lobbyists or TV political ads, it appears as coming from some innocuously named source dripping in false patriotism.

Evidence of the presence of dark money and the extent of the shadow that it casts over American politics is revealed in a study where by 2006, gray and dark money from outside money sources (i.e. PACS, Super PACs, wealthy individuals, corporations, and non-profit fronts) across 6 states, representing $1/5^{th}$ of the American population, accounted for 59% of the money channeled into campaigns , and by 2011 only 29% of the outside money was fully transparent. (Long) A singular example of the extent the very wealthy are willing to go to buy America are the Koch brothers who have a net worth of $42.9 billion dollars and who budgeted $889 million dollars for the 2016 election. (Confessore) In the words of our own billionaire president, "I gave to many people, before this two months ago. I was a businessman. I gave to everyone, everybody. When they called, I gave. And do you know what? When I needed something from them, years later, I call them, they are there for me. And that's a broken system." – President Donald Trump

The End of the Road – The Supreme Court of Elders

Even if somehow we were able to overcome these walls upon walls of obstruction to government by the people and pass legislation that reflect the will of the people, we would only come to the final dead end and the most undemocratic of all our institutions of governance, the Supreme Court, a Puritan Court of Elders that we appointed for life and can declare the will of the people unconstitutional based on a Constitution that is treated like the Bible and the signatories as the Apostles even though we know that at its inception the Bible was a democracy only for the elect.

What is True Democracy?

First let us define true democracy by what it is not. When we are advocating true democracy, we are not talking about the pale and anemic form of democracy that we have been discussing where the political system was at its inception conceived and organized to thwart the will and power of the American people. Nor are we referring to the classic neo-liberal philosophy of democracy that rationalizes a view of human nature and the role of government that undermines the reality of man as a social being and advocates a deformed concept of democracy that is more about securing induvial rights and freedoms and keeping people apart rather than bringing them together. In this form of democracy there is no such thing as "We the People of the United States" or as Benjamin Barber asserts in a brilliant study on the character and nature of liberal democracy and the need for participation politics,

> "Pluralism is advocated not in the name of the intrinsic merits of diversity but because there can be no common or public ends, no common or public goods, no common or public will. Commonality itself is transformed into an enemy of doubt and thus into the nemesis of freedom. The impossibility of certain knowledge becomes the impossibility of affirmative politics; without an agreement on common principles and common thought, there can be no common life. The only commonality there is in politics [in the United States] is the commonality of individual interests, a form of collective selfishness that only holds together if the group serves the individual's self-interest." (Barber 62)

In this deformed idealization of the individual, there is no social sense of empathy, no sense of self-sacrifice beyond our individual children, and, even there, the divorce rate belies even the most fundamental nucleus of our shared being. There is no sense of the transcendent spirit embodied in our collective history and culture. When the United States was breaking away from the oppressive class system and social conformity of European feudalism, the freeing of the individual was the dynamo of freedom that was a significant factor in the rapid growth of the United States, and throughout our history our emphasis on individual freedom has contributed much to what is good about us, our uniqueness, our creativity, innovativeness, and our energy, but as Aristotle's brilliant concept of the golden mean would teach us, every virtue in excess is a vice, and, at this point in time in our history, our glorification of the individual at the expense of our social being has degenerated into narcissism, cancerous cells feeding off of healthy cells in the body politic, leaving us all alone, defenseless against the butcher shop called the corporate state. As Robert Nesbit in *Quest for Community* noted,

> "The genius of totalitarian leadership lies in its profound awareness that personalities can't tolerate moral isolation, and absolute and relentless power will be acceptable only where it comes to be seen as the only available form of community and membership." – Robert Nesbit
>
> We see that the repression of one half of our being has manifested itself in a society gone mad and that the only way to cure ourselves of this imbalance of the body politic is to follow the path to true democracy, a path that passes through two pillars that hold up the dream of a society by the people, for the people, and of the people. These two pillars are Freedom and Responsibility. Together they are the key to a well-balanced body politic and a new form of being in the evolution of the human spirit that is at one with itself, and every cell, every one of us contains the whole, and the whole contains the will and the dreams of each and every one of us, a dream that transcends time and place, a dream of immortality.
>
> "Democracy is a revolution that has never been won," but it dwells in the heart of the American dream and is rooted in our finest values and traditions. To realize this dream, we envision two major changes in the American political and economic system.

In Part Three of this manifesto, we will introduce Phase One of the New American Revolution, a government by the people implemented through direct political democracy manifested in the initiative, referendum, and recall process at all levels of government acting as a check and balance against a system that in its present form is a government of, by, and for the vampire class and the living dead that serve them. Phase Two of the New American Revolution will introduce a new paradigm of economic democracy where the American people will go in partnership with American labor, and we turn capitalism on its head. In Phase Three of the New American Revolution we will lay out the plan to make the dream real in a how-to- manual of revolution.

PART THREE: Government by the People

Illustration #16

Government by the People

When we use the term, "true democracy," politically, we are referring to citizen legislation and the direct participation of the American people in the political process. Some people call it "direct democracy" or "participatory democracy," but we call it true democracy, pure and simple, because anything else is a watered-down version of the original meaning of the term. Fortunately, we have a long tradition of true democracy in the United States, and the best manifestations of this tradition are to be found in the initiative, referendum, and recall process of direct citizen legislation.

In general terms, an *initiative* is an instrument by which a citizen or citizen groups can introduce legislation to be voted on by the electorate, and if the voters approve the initiative, it becomes law. There are two types of referendums, a direct and an indirect referendum. In a *direct referendum* when a citizen or citizen group disapprove of a law passed by the local, state, or national legislative body, they can introduce a referendum to be voted on by the electorate. If the electorate approves the referendum, the law is repealed. An *indirect referendum*, on the other hand, is how the legislators by a majority vote can refer a bill to the general electorate to be voted on and confirmed. The *recall* is a democratic means by which we can make elected officials continually accountable to the electorate. If a citizen or citizen group are convinced that an elected official has not been representative of the people's will or that the elected official is unfit for office, they can introduce a petition to recall that official. If the electorate approve the recall, the elected official is dismissed from his or her elected position. These instruments of direct citizen legislation and participation in the political process became a significant part of the democratic revolution of the Populist and Progressive Era in the United States.

The Populist and Progressive Revolution

The Populist and Progressive era of the 1880s and the early 1900s looked very much like the United States of today. The Robber Barons of the Gilded Age, like the vampire capitalist of today, fed off small famers, impoverished the urban working class, and exploited immigrant and cheap child labor. Like today, big money and big business corrupted the body politic at all levels and created, then as they have today, a one-dollar-one-vote system of government where there were large giveaways of land and money to privately owned railroads and other corporations that fed off of the common wealth in what was then as now a massive corporate welfare state. Large trusts and monopolies and oligarchies of the period mirrored the behavior of our modern day global corporations, and it was then that corporations were adjudicated as legal "persons" and became the Leviathans that play a major role in the horror story we are experiencing today.

The Populist and Progressive movements of the 1880 and early 1900s spearheaded the revolt against the vampire capitalism of that era and fought for the inclusion of the initiative, referendum, and recall process of direct and participatory democracy in city charters and state constitutions. Because of their efforts Nebraska in 1897 became the first state to allow cities to place initiatives and referendums in their charters. One year later, the citizens of South Dakota copied the initiative and referendum provisions from the 1848 Swiss Constitution and on November 5, 1898, South Dakota became the first state to adopt a statewide initiative and popular referendum process. Utah followed in 1900, and Oregon voters approved an initiative and referendum amendment to their constitution by a 11-1 margin in 1902. Other states followed. In 1906 Montana voters approved an initiative and popular direct referendum amendment proposed by the state legislature. Oklahoma became the first state to provide for the initiative and popular referendum in its original constitution in 1907, and Maine and Michigan passed an initiative and direct referendum amendment in 1908. In 1911 California placed an initiative and direct popular referendum in their constitution. Other states were to follow, and by 1918, 24 states and numerous cities had adopted the initiative and direct popular referendum.

Through the use of the initiative, referendum, and recall process as an instrument of democratic change the Populists and the Progressives with limited funds but a vast army of volunteers were able to initiate and pioneer legislation and a vision of America that led to the enactment of anti-trust laws, the first income tax (a 5% tax on the income of the rich), a constitutional change that allowed the American people to vote directly for their Senators for the first time, and the right to vote for women. They also set the agenda for the New Deal of shared prosperity, a progressive income tax, social security, an inheritance tax, the regulation of the stock market, and the recognition of labor's right to organize.

This is not to say that he initiative, referendum, and recall process favors one ideology or party over another. It doesn't. It expresses the will of the people over time. For example, during the 1980s and 1990s the results of initiatives, referendums, and recalls across the country showed a decided shift to a more conservative and Republican expression of the will of the people as exemplified by the tax revolt and Proposition 13 that capped property taxes in California at 3%.

However, as noted earlier, we are looking more like we looked during the Populist and Progressive Era, and the American people are beginning to stir again as reflected in the fact that more states are amending their constitutions to include the initiative, referendum, and recall process as part of their constitutions. In 1868 Wyoming voters adopted the initiative and referendum process in their constitution, and in 1972 Florida adopted a statewide initiative. Mississippi in 1992 restored the initiative process to their constitution and became the latest state to adopt this valuable instrument of direct democracy, but the movement has not stopped there. More and more citizens are demanding citizen law making, and more people are beginning to ask, "What is an initiative, referendum, and recall?" When it is explained to them, they say, "Really? We can do that?"

To be expected, as interest grows, the antidemocratic forces in America have become more vocal in their opposition and criticism of direct democracy. They argue that the initiative, referendum, and recall process of direct citizen lawmaking tramples on the rights of minorities, that big money controls the process more so than it does representative government, and the people are not informed enough nor intelligent an educated enough to make and repeal laws. Direct democracy is mob rule, they say, dominated by the passions of the moment and the mass movement of the herd led by democratic demigods and charlatans. Fortunately, we have over a hundred years of history and experience with the initiative, referendum, and recall process in the United States and as many years of records, results, and research. American has been the pioneer in direct citizen lawmaking and the laboratory for direct democracy, so let's look at the criticisms of the process of citizen law making in the light of the fact.

Does Big Money Dominate the Initiative, Referendum, and Recall Process?

Critics argue that big money dominates the initiative, referendum, and recall process. We will reframe that accusation in the form of a question that asks, can big money and wealthy special interest groups and/or individuals buy the initiative, referendum and recall process of citizen lawmaking in the same way that they can buy influence in Washington? The answer is no. Elizabeth Gerber in her book, *The Popular Paradox: Interest Group Influence and the Promise of Direct Democracy,* 1999, conducted an extensive surveys of the activities and motivations of interest groups and analyzed campaign records from 161 direct legislative campaigns in eight states and observed that wealthy economic interest groups are less successful than broad based popular citizen groups in getting initiatives passed.

> An analysis of 57 ballots measured between 1988 and 1992 reveals that only 31% of initiatives backed by wealthy economic interest groups passed, in contrast to a 50% success rate for propositions backed by broad based popular citizen groups. Gerber's research was supported by a study by Shaun Bowler and Todd Donovan where they found while 40% of all initiatives on the California ballot from 1986 to 1996 passed, only 14% of the initiatives passed that were supported and funded by special interests. (Sabato 174)
>
> However, narrow based, wealthy economic interest groups are more successful and defeating propositions that they oppose. This is reflected in how narrow based economic interest groups spend their money in initiative campaigns. According to the Public Policy Institute of California, between 1981 and 1990, economic interests spent over 78% of their $99 million in contributions to defeat ballot measure. During the same period, citizen groups spent 88% of their $33 million to support proposed changes to the status quo. (Gerber, Interest Group Influence)

This is reflected in the following charts. (Gerber 17-18)

Initiative Passage Rates by Source of Majority Support	
Source of Majority Support	Passage Rate, %
Economic	22
Citizen	60

Initiative Failure Rates by Source of Majority Opposition	
Source of Majority Opposition	Failure Rate, %
Economic	58
Citizen	59

Chart #14

Economic special interest groups are successful in opposing propositions for many reasons, but at the heart of the strategy is the campaign to confuse the voters. Initiative voters have been found to be essentially circumspect. If they do not understand a proposition, they will generally vote no or not vote at all. Special interest economic interests will try to exploit this virtue through deceptive advertisement and the introduction of competing propositions that confuse the issue and lengthen the ballot to further confuse the voters with the volume of information that they must absorb. This pouring of money into a campaign to oppose it, however, is a double-edged-blade. For example, studies indicate that the more money that is spent on advertisement, the more the public becomes aware of the proposition, and in many instances the ad campaign does not affect how they vote, it affects their interest in the campaign and causes them to become more informed. Also, studies indicate that if the issues in a proposition are critical to the average citizen, the more money that is poured into the campaign, the more likely that even if the initiative is initially defeated, the issues will appear over and over again in new initiatives until the labyrinth of lies is exposed to the light of day.

Money has always influenced the initiative process and will continue to be an obstacle to the free expression of the will of the people through the initiative, referendum, and recall process, but the fact still remains that broad based popular citizen groups have been successful advancing their agenda and the people's choice about 50% of the time. Using a baseball analogue, It is better to be batting .500 in the initiative, referendum, and recall process than it is to never get up to the plate in Washington where economic special interests know it is easier to bribe and pay off a couple hundred representatives or a couple of representatives on a Congressional committee than it is to bribe the entire voting population of the United States of America or even one state. A million dollars goes a long way in Washington, but it's not even a dollar-a-vote in California or Washington State.

> Finally, if we had an initiative, referendum, and recall process at every level of our government, it would act as a as a check against a representative system that does not represent the will of the people by just being there. The process of citizen lawmaking and oversight is like a presidential veto, its mere existence effects the behavior of our representatives in the United States Congress and our state and local governments. Like the Sword of Damocles, it is ever present as a warning against the excesses of greed, corruption, and influence peddling. With true democracy as a check and balance against a representative system of government that does not represent the will of the people, the American people do not have to go to the streets in order to protest, they can turn out at the voting booth to pass or repeal legislation that will be responsive to their needs. For example, do you think that if we had a national initiative, referendum, and recall process that the United States that Congress could have passed the recent tax cut that overwhelmingly favored the top 1% of the population in income? Never.

Does the Initiative, Referendum, and Recall Process Trample Minority Rights?

Critics also argue that the initiative referendum, and recall process undermine minority rights. From the inception of this country there was a concern for minority rights versus the will of the majority. In recent years the initiative and referendum process has become so popular in states like California that this concern for minority rights has become highlighted by critics of the process who point out the most prejudicial uses of the initiative, referendum, and recall process in the past such as the constitutional amendment in 1920 that essentially barred Japanese aliens from owning land, Proposition 187 that was passed in 1994 and reduced social services to illegal immigrants, and Proposition 209 that eliminated affirmative action programs in public education, government hiring, and contracting. So, let us look at the record.

California is particularly interesting as a study in minority rights versus the will of the majority. California has become a majority-minority state, meaning that no single ethnic or racial group constitutes a simple majority in the state. However, even though non-Hispanic whites are no longer a majority in the state, they still make up two-thirds of the voting population, and in a winner-take-all voting process, they can potentially outvote and pass legislation that ethnic and racial minorities in California collectively opposed. This being the case, the question of whether or not minorities are winners or losers in the initiative, referendum, and recall process becomes critical, not only for blacks, Asians, and Latinos in California, but for whites as well since they may soon become a minority and are now a minority in some cities, counties, and districts of the country. As the movement for true democracy in this country picks up speed, the issue of minority versus majority rights has become an important issue to us all.

> In 2001, Zoltan Haynal and Hugh Louch published a study for the Public Policy Institute of California entitled, *Are There Winners and Losers?* This study was based on the analysis of all initiatives between 1978 and 2002 in California. The study concluded that even though minorities did not fare well on minority focused propositions like Proposition 187 and Proposition 209 referred to previously, these types of propositions only represent about 5% of all the propositions considered during the period studied.

When we consider the full scope of the propositions considered between 1978 and 2000, and, at the same time, consider propositions that minorities say are important to them or, as a group, they have a clear preference for or against, the results of the study concludes that blacks, Latinos, and Asians have roughly the same probability of being on the winning side of an initiative as do white voters. (Hajnal 22-24)

Initiative Are Popular with All Racial and Ethnic Groups

Best way to address California's problems?	White	Asian	Latino	Black
Citizen's initiatives	76	73	83	92
Governor/legislature	24	27	18	8

SOURCE: PPIC Statewide Survey, January 2000

Chart #15

I think it is obvious why African Americans, Asians, Latinos, and most working-class Californians support the initiative, referendum, and recall process. Like the vast majority of Americans, they know that Sacramento and Washington are dominated by big money, global corporations and financial institutions, and special interest groups, and it far better to be batting .500 in the initiative process than never getting up to the plate in Washington and Sacramento. In a CBS/New York Times Poll, the question was asked, "Would you say the government is pretty much run by a few big interests looking out for themselves or that it is run for the benefit of all the people?" In the poll, 64% of the respondents said that the government was run by a few big interests and 28% of the respondents said it was run by all the people with 8% unsure. In the same poll, the respondents were asked, "How much say do you think people like yourself have about what the government does – a good deal or not much?" In the poll 90% of the respondents said that they did not think that people like themselves had a good deal to say about what the government does. Is it a wonder that the initiative, referendum, and recall process is so popular today? In California, the 1990s alone accounted for almost a quarter of all the initiatives that California's voters have ever voted on since 1911 when the process was first made a part of California's constitution. (CBS/New York Times Poll, July 11-15, 2004)

Does the Initiative, Referendum, and Recall Process Work for Everyone?

Though the Hajnal and Louch study focused primarily on ethnicity and race, the study also highlighted other important demographic data and information related to the voting patterns in the initiative, referendum a recall process. The study noted that the biggest changes in who are winners and losers had less to do with race and ethnicity than it did with liberal and conservative politics, Democrats and Republicans. Liberals and Democrats were regular winners in the 80s, but in the 90s Democrats have been 2% less likely to win than Republicans, and liberals have slipped 6% over the last decade. However, what makes the process remarkable is that it not only transcends race and ethnic origins or minority politics, but it also transcends the simple-minded choices of winner-takes-all two-party politics and elections by demanding that voters make decisions issue by issue. When given a choice, issue by issue, the American people can't be simply categorized along party lines. This observation of voter behavior has been supported by a study done by David Magleby in 1984, *Direct Legislation: Voting on Ballot Propositions in the United States*, Baltimore, MD: John Hopkins University Press.

> In that study, Magleby's research shows that voters tend to support or oppose propositions independent of their party affiliations. On some issues they will vote conservative or along Republican Party lines, but on other issues the same voter will vote liberal or along Democratic Party line or maybe somewhere else on the political spectrum. This leads us to conclude that the simple minded breakdown of the American people into a two party system does not reflect the true interest or the full scope of their will and that direct citizen lawmaking, issue by issue, is a far better way to determine public policy and avoid polarization and the reduction of choices to a winner-take-all vote for a candidate who then takes away from you your freedom of choice for a designated term of office. "Yes," you may say, "but we can vote them out." However, that is like saying to a bank robber that he can't go back into the bank after he has stolen all the money. (Magleby)

Finally, what is most remarkable about the study by Hajnal and Louch is that they observed that - as with party affiliation, race, and ethnicity - regardless of age, residence, income, or education, the voters will be a winner over fifty percent of the time. These results by Hajnal and Louch are illustrated in the following table that was compiled from the authors calculation of data from the Los Angeles Times exit polls. (Hajnal 31)

Percentage Voting for the Winning Side:
All Propositions, Raw Numbers

Group	%
White	60.8
Black	55.6
Latino	56.3
Asian	56.1
Upper Income	60.1
Lower Income	59.2
College degree	58.5
No high school diploma	58.0
Under age 30	59.2
Over age 65	60.3
Bay Area	58.0
Central Valley	60.8
Los Angeles	59.1
Republican	63.2
Democrat	58.8
Conservative	62.9
Liberal	54.7

SOURCE: Authors' calculations from the *Los Angeles Times* exit polls.

Chart #16

I repeat for emphasis. Regardless of race, ethnicity, party affiliation, age, residence, income, or education all voters through the initiative, referendum, and recall process of citizen lawmaking win fifty percent of the time. This is a major advanced over the political system as we know it today and represents a major step towards a truly democratic society.

Is the Average American Capable of Being a Citizen Lawmaker?

Thomas Jefferson is quoted as saying,

> "Men in their makeup are naturally divided into two camps, those who fear and distrust the people and wish to draw all power from them into the hands of higher classes, and those who identify themselves with the people, have confidence in them, cherish and consider them the safest and most honest, if although not the most wise, depository of public intent."

He then went on to ask, "Who will govern the governors?" And his answer was "There is only one force in the nation that can be depended upon to keep the government pure and the governors honest, and that is the people themselves. They alone, if well informed, can prevent the corruption of power, and restore the nation to its rightful course if it should go astray. They alone are the safest depository of the ultimate power of government."

As Jefferson predicted, there are those who argue against direct and participatory democracy. They argue that the average American is not capable of self-government. They lack the education to make informed judgements and determine their own self-interest, and they are easily manipulated by their passions and prejudices. They call direct democracy "election anarchy," "lousy lawmaking," "democracy's barrier to racial equality," and "the right of the American people to make fools of themselves." They point out some of the most wrong-headed propositions passed through the initiative process as proof of the folly of allowing the American people to make decisions for themselves, but how can you argue that the American people are not capable of making decisions for themselves, yet, they are capable of choosing their own representative that will make decisions for them? How are examples of laws passed through the initiative and referendum process any more repugnant than similarly repugnant example of laws passed by our legislatures? They are not, and, basically, it is an argument that focuses on the wrong criteria. The question should be, Is the average American voter capable of making an informed and reasoned decision about propositions that are presented to them through the initiative, referendum and recall process that not only serves their own individual interests but also serves the common good?

The notion that the American people are not informed enough to make policy decisions is not supported by the data. Voters are risk adverse, and if presented with a proposition that they do not fully understand, or have doubts about, or some confusion over the proposition, they are likely to settle on the stability of the status quo and vote against the proposition. On the other hand, if they sufficiently understand the proposition based on information available, they will evaluate the cost/gain to them, and they will vote, yes, even if the proposition involves some risk but serves their interest, ideology, or simply what they believe to be right or wrong or better for the country.

The study by Shaun Bowler and Todd Donovan, *Demanding Choices*, observes that the voter will make these decisions based on information available through (1) peer groups, (2) relatives, (3) their own experience, (4) information available through the media, debates, special interest groups, leaders, and organizations that the voter identifies with and trust, (5) pamphlets mailed by the government to every registered voter that in most cases include a copy of the proposition, the arguments in favor and against the proposition written by the major supporters and major opponent of the proposition, and a list of key individuals and organizations that support or oppose the proposition. (Bowler)

The pamphlets issued by most of the cities and states are of particular importance as a source of information because they are issued to all the registered voters, and they are very popular with the voters as a source of information. The extent of the use of the pamphlet as a source of information was the subject of a study at the University of California at Davis by Dubois, Feeney, and Constantine. The study revealed that only 20% of the respondents claimed to have read the actual text of the proposition being voted on, yet, more that 90% of the respondents claimed to have looked at the arguments in favor and against the proposition in the pamphlet, and more than 80% claimed that the names of the organizations and individuals listed in the pamphlet who were for or against the proposition was important to them in making a decision on how to vote. (Dubois, Philip 58-59). The study also observed that the ballot pamphlet was the most frequent source of information cited by the least educated voters, and even with limited information, processing, and reading skills this segment of the population were quite capable of coming to a reasoned decision that clearly reflected an understanding of the proposition, and its impact on them.

If then, based on this studies and others, we accept the conclusion of years of research that the average American voter, is quite capable of being sufficiently informed and that they are quite capable of understanding the impact of the proposition on their own interests, the next question becomes, Is the average American voter easily manipulated by their passions, prejudices, and narrow self-interest, and, therefore, they are not capable of the far sighted, broad mindedness, deliberative decision making and judgement of their betters?

This claim that the average American voter is not capable of going beyond their own prejudices and narrow self-interest is blatantly false, and it is also narrow-minded and biased in its indifference to the plight of the average working American. In fact, it is often demonstrated that the body politic is less disconnected than the elite classes. In fact, it can be argued that academics in their studies put too much emphasis on what distinguishes them, education and so-called objectivity where, in fact, the intelligence of the elite classes is often used to find infinite ways to rationalize the irrational, and what they call objectivity is a way to distance themselves from the pain they cause, whereas the average American is on the leading edge of the consequences of bad law. They are the nerve ends of the body politics, and they know that something is not working because it hurts.

In addition, the average American voter has also proven repeatedly that they can transcend their own pain and empathize with the pain of others and understand the boarder implications of their responsibilities as citizens. This is revealed in the study of tax propositions. If your average American voter was as narrow minded in their self-interest as their critics would lead us to believe, we would expect the average American voter to vote again propositions that would raise taxes and vote for propositions that would lower taxes regardless of the broader consequences of their vote, but that is not the case. In a study by Bill Piper sponsored by the Initiative and Referendum Institute entitled, *"A Brief Analysis of Vote Behavior Regarding Tax Initiative From 1928 to March 2000,* It was observed in the study that, based on analysis of the history of tax initiatives, the evidence confirms that voters are quite restrained in making decisions about taxation. The record shows that most anti-tax initiatives fail and that the voters do approve tax increases when they feel that the tax increase is necessary. For example, between 1978 and March 2000 there were 131 tax initiatives and only 51 passed, a number that represents 39% of the tax initiatives voted on by the voters in this period. Of the initiative that were passed, there was only a 10% difference in approval between anti-tax initiatives and pro-tax initiative.(Piper 4) To further demonstrate the reasonableness of the voters it should be noted that the most popular form of tax revolt was to index taxes to inflation so that a taxpayer's tax burden would not increase even though real income had not increase. One of the prime example of taxes and the average American's ability to see beyond themselves is the fact that older citizens voters without children attending schools are not more likely to oppose school tax referendums (Bowler pg. 95), and this is true of other forms of initiatives and referendums where the average citizen will define his or her own economic interests in terms of the common good and vote for propositions that express empathy, social responsibility, and just good common sense.

> No, the American people are not the problem. The problem is the vampire class who can't see their own image in the mirror. They see the idealized image of themselves created by the media and story tellers in their pay who project on them an image of being far sighted, broadminded, deliberate, and fair. Emotionally, they are projected as civil, considerate, and tolerant. On the other hand, in the mirror in which they can't see their own image, they project their real nature and character onto us. With blood on their lips, they see us as vulgar, rude, and uncivilized. They are responsible for the death of millions, and they consider us as impulsive, irrational, and prone to aggressive outbursts. They see us as the mob incapable of self-rule, yet, in fact, the real mob is in Washington, on Wall Street, and in the boardrooms of corporate America. It is interesting that the prejudices that they project on the majority of the American people is quite like those depicting women and racial and ethnic minorities as being childish, irrational, ignorant, irresponsible etc. They do this so that they don't have to face the truth of who they really are in all their ugliness, and they do it to protect themselves from you and me, because if we did see them for who they really are, we would probably become that mob that they fear and tear them apart.

We're the Solution, Not the Problem

No, the American people are not the problem. We are the solution, and a true political and economic democracy is the mirror and the lamp that will enlighten us and enable us to see the true image of who they are and who we are, and it will be a much different picture. Therefore, we demand the initiative, referendum, and recall process of direct and participatory democracy be incorporated into the American political system at all levels of government. We also demand a constitutional amendment that will enable the American people to directly amend the Constitution of the United States. However, this is only half the story. We can't have a true democracy when we spend most of our waking hours working in a totalitarian state called the job working for the Boss. Therefore, in part two of the new American revolution we will focus on economic democracy and an economy by, for, and of the people.

PART FOUR: How They Control Us

> "We may congratulate ourselves that this cruel war is nearing its end. It has cost a vast amount of treasure and blood...It has indeed been a trying hour for the Republic, but I see in the near future, a crisis approaching that unnerves me and causes one to tremble for the safety of my country. As a result of the war, corporations have been enthroned and an era of corruption in high places will follow, and the money power of the country will endeavor to prolong its reign by working upon the prejudices of the people until all wealth is aggregated in a few hands and the Republic is destroyed. I feel at this moment more anxiety for the safety of my country than ever before, even in the midst of war. God grant that my suspicions may prove groundless."
> – Abraham Lincoln.

I Ask You? Who Would Vote for This in a True Democracy?

If we was a true democracy, would we vote for an economic system that has the highest levels of income and wealth inequality in the industrial world, and, at the same time, has the lowest levels of social mobility of any developed country except the United Kingdom and Italy? Or in other words, would you vote for an economic system where 20% of the population controls 80% of the wealth and income in the country, and 10% of the population own it all?

If this was a true democracy, would we vote for an economic system where the heirs to the Walmart fortune are paid $1.56 million dollars an hour for doing nothing except for having been born, while at the same time, Walmart employees make $7 dollars an hour? And this is only one example of the emerging aristocracy of inherited wealth and power in America that is passing our life blood on from one generation to another, feeding off us even when we are dead.

If this was a true democracy, would we vote for an economic system where corporations are wealthier and more powerful than most nation states, and, despite the fact that they dwarf the average American, they are recognized as legal "persons" with the same rights and freedoms as you and me as citizens of the United States, but they have none of the responsibilities, and they are devoid of any feelings or empathy? Would you vote for an economic system dominated by these Frankenstein like Leviathans that are certifiably insane sociopaths capable of committing mass murder?

If this was a true democracy, would you vote for an economic system that at its heart is about blood sacrifice, and its ultimate expression of "creative destruction" is the massive bloodletting of war where millions upon millions are sacrificed just to keep the system going?

If this was a true democracy, would you vote for an economic system that must continually grow or it will die and has become a cancerous growth that is consuming the planet, forcing every living thing into decline? Forests are shrinking, water tablets falling, soil eroding, wetlands disappearing, fisheries collapsing, range land deteriorating, rivers running dry, temperatures rising, coral reefs dying, and plant and animal species disappearing. Bottom line, would you vote for and economic system that is killing us all?

So, what is the economic alternative to mass suicide? In part one of the New American Revolution we outlined a blueprint for a political revolution that will transform politics in America and give the American people the instrumentality to transform our economy into an economic democracy. So, what is an economic democracy of the people by the people and for the people? To understand what an economic democracy is, we must first understand what it isn't. We must understand how vampire capitalism controls our economy and why previous attempts at reform have failed.

We the People Pay

In our tax laws and codes, private property that generates income cannot be taxed. The loss of value from wear and tear, the obsolescence and renewal of profit producing property (i.e. buildings, machinery, office equipment, informational and communications systems, transportation facilities, and vehicles etc.) is written off, depreciated over time, and can be deducted from corporate and business income. At the same time, that same profit producing property can be used as collateral when corporations seek out new capital investment and corporate loans. Which is to say, that we the people of the United States as taxpayers pay for the growth and renewal of the corporate Leviathans that feed off us. (Gates 100-102) A good example of how the vampire capitalists can grow rich simply by manipulating the laws governing depreciation is the real estate boom of the 1980s. In 1980, office buildings constructed during that year could be written off over a 45 year period, whereas, in 1981, in a political giveaway in the name of free enterprise, the Reagan administration changed the laws governing depreciation and enabled corporations to write off the cost of construction in 15 years. As a result of that tax giveaway, it is estimated that the change in the depreciation provision of the tax law cost the American people at least $143 billion dollars in lost tax revenues. (Easterbrook)

Well, you could say that corporations will have to pay corporate income tax on revenues generated by the profit producing properties that the American people are paying for by allowing corporations and business to deduct the cost of the means of production from their income tax. Not so, the blood in the form of taxes that flows into the body politic so as to create, support, develop, and maintain the infrastructure of the United States of America (i.e. the roads, the airways and waterways, the utilities, the information and communications network, the educational system, public and environmental health and conservation services, law enforcement, and the military etc.) does not come, for the most part, from taxes on corporate income.

Since the 1950s, corporations have paid an increasingly smaller share of the overall federal tax revenues. After World War Two, corporate taxes accounted for 28% of federal revenues. By 1993, corporate taxes fell to 9.3%.In 2019, the United States collected 1.1% of GDP in corporate income tax. This is the lowest since the 1930s, and, compared to all the advanced economies in the Organization of Economic Cooperation and Development, it's the lowest, with one exception, Latvia. Overall, if we factor in the tax loopholes and special exemptions and subsides for corporations, it becomes clear that we have a corporate welfare state in America where corporations are on the dole and pay zero taxes or very little compared to the average American citizen. (Furman 2) For example, a report from the Institute on Taxation and Economic Policy determined that 60 profitable corporations listed among the Fortune 500 companies paid zero dollars in federal income taxes and enjoyed a total of $4.3 billion dollars in federal rebates combined. That adds up to a 5.5.% negative corporate tax, and the list includes companies like Amazon, Delta, General Motors, Molson/Coors, and other well-known names. Based on the same study, another 56 companies paid an effective tax rate between 0% and

5% on their 2018 income with an effective rate of 2.2.% combined. (Institute on Taxation and Economic Policy https://itep.org/corporate-tax-avoidance-in-the-first-year-of-the-rump-tax-laws)

FEDERAL INCOME TAX RATES FOR 379 COMPANIES, 2018
($ in billions of dollars)

Effective Tax Rate Group	# of companies	% of companies	Profit	Tax	Average Rate
Less than 10.5%	195	51	$322	$6	2%
10.5% to 21%	127	34	$346	$55	16%
More than 21%	57	15	$98	$26	27%
All 379 companies	379	100	$766	$87	11%
144 Ultra-lowtax companies					
0% or less	91	24	$101	$-6	-6%
0% to 5%	56	14	$103	$2	2%

SOURCE: Institute of Taxation and Economic Policy analisys of corporate of 10-K filings Created with Datawrapper

Chart #17

The defenders of free market capitalism argue that the 1% who own the majority of stock and the CEOs and other high paid functionaries in the corporate system that profit the most from the write offs and low corporate taxes, have to pay personal income tax, and that money as blood flows back into the body politic and contributes to the health of the American economic system. Not so, individual tax rates have followed the same path as corporate income taxes. For the year 1955, the effective tax rate for the top 1% of the population was 86% and the effective tax rate for the average middle-class family was below 10%. In 2000, the effective federal tax rate for the top 1 % of the population was 34%, and the effective tax rate for the average middle-class family was 19%. Add to that the fact that most state and local taxes are regressive and often are flat taxes, penalties, and fines, it is estimated that the average taxpayer's tax rate is approximately the same as the top 1%. This is just a part of how the vampire capitalists bleed the body politic through their control of the political system and the economy.

Historical Highest Marginal Income Tax Rates

Year	Top Marginal Rate	Year	Top Marginal Rate	Year	Top Marginal Rate
1913	7.0%	1946	86.45%	1979	70.00%
1914	7.0%	1947	86.45%	1980	70.00%
1915	7.0%	1948	82.13%	1981	69.13%
1916	15.0%	1949	82.13%	1982	50.00%
1917	67.0%	1950	91.00%	1983	50.00%
1918	77.0%	1951	91.00%	1984	50.00%
1919	73.0%	1952	92.00%	1985	50.00%
1920	73.0%	1953	92.00%	1986	50.00%
1921	73.0%	1954	91.00%	1987	38.50%
1922	56.0%	1955	91.00%	1988	28.00%
1923	56.0%	1956	91.00%	1989	28.00%
1924	46.0%	1957	91.00%	1990	31.00%
1925	25.0%	1958	91.00%	1991	31.00%
1926	25.0%	1959	91.00%	1992	31.00%
1927	25.0%	1960	91.00%	1993	39.60%
1928	25.0%	1961	91.00%	1994	39.60%
1929	24.0%	1962	91.00%	1995	39.60%
1930	25.0%	1963	91.00%	1996	39.60%
1931	25.0%	1964	77.00%	1997	39.60%
1932	63.0%	1965	70.00%	1998	39.60%
1933	63.0%	1966	70.00%	1999	39.60%
1934	63.0%	1967	70.00%	2000	39.60%
1935	63.0%	1968	75.25%	2001	38.60%
1936	79.0%	1969	77.00%	2002	38.60%
1937	79.0%	1970	71.75%	2003	35.00%
1938	79.0%	1971	70.00%	2004	35.00%
1939	79.0%	1972	70.00%	2005	35.00%
1940	81.10%	1973	70.00%	2006	35.00%
1941	81.00%	1974	70.00%	2007	35.00%
1942	88.00%	1975	70.00%	2008	35.00%
1943	88.00%	1976	70.00%	2009	35.00%
1944	94.00%	1977	70.00%	2010	35.00%
1945	94.00%	1978	70.00%	2011	35.00%

Chart #18

How the Vampire Capitalist Control What We Think and What We Think About

In a society that still has the bare remnants of a republican form of government and the fragments of a democracy that could possibly be the instrument of change around which the American people could rally and challenge the basic institution of the system that oppresses them, it is important that the interests of the capitalist class be well articulated and supported by arguments and fake facts and data that will make vampire capitalism and the value system of greed and lust for blood appear to serve the general interest of the consumer, the consumed, and the electorate.

An important means to this end has been the support by the wealthiest individuals in the country of tax-free foundations such as the Ford Foundation, the Rockefeller Foundation, the Carnegie Foundation, and radical right wing foundations such as the Bradley Foundation and the Olin Foundation. These foundations pour money into think tanks and round table discussion groups ranging from the moderately conservative Brookings Institute, Rand Corporation, and the Council of Foreign Relations to the more radical right wing think tanks like the Hoover Institution, the Cato Institution, and the American Enterprise Institute. These institutes undertake policy research, draw up model legislation, bring together representatives from the business community, government officials, respectable non-radical academics, and members of the media to debate, discuss, and refine policy and strategies to protect and further their common interests.

A good example of how money determines how and what we think is the Council on Foreign Relations. The Council holds frequent meetings and dinners which feature a guest speaker, usually a Washington or foreign "statesman." The meetings and dinners are held behind closed doors, and everything said is off the record with violations of this code of silence being grounds for dismissal from the Council. Through early 1988, out of this group, has come 14 secretaries of state, 14 treasury secretaries, 11 defense secretaries, and a score of other federal department heads. Historian Arthur Schlesinger Jr. called the Council on Foreign Affairs a "front organization" for "the heart of the American Establishment." David Halberstam, the author of *The Best and the Brightest* is quoted as saying that the businessmen who attend the meetings and dinners "walk in one door as acquisitive businessmen and come out another door as statesmen figures."(Campbell 48) But this is not the end.

How the Vampire Capitalists Control Our Hopes and Dreams

Illustration #17

> As noted, six media Leviathans control 90% of all we read, watch, and listen to. Their power goes far beyond the news and editorials that are fabricated by the foundations, think tanks, and the establishment scholars and pundits. From the cradle to the grave the media giants control the fairytales and lullabies, the movies and the TV shows, the books and the magazines we read, and the music we listen to. They create the stories that give our life meaning and define the roles we will play in life. They control the one force that they fear the most – our creativity, our ability to hope and dream, our ability to make things real, and our ability to go beyond ourselves and create a future.

What the media Leviathans are doing today reminds me of a story that an anthropologist who specialized in Mexico told me years ago about what gypsies in Mexico did when they went to isolated villages before TV. The gypsies would show a free movie on the white washed walls of the local church, and while the peasants from the village were watching the movies, escaping from the hardships of their daily life, imaging to be someone else, the gypsies would pick their pockets of what little money they had.

> Today, the white-washed-walls of the church are the TV screens where, for example, millions upon millions of Americans watch the National Football League, the games and sports-shows; and they fantasize about being the Boss who buys and sells the million-dollar slaves who play the game. As the make-believe-Boss, they argue incessantly about who they should buy and sell, and when they watch the game, they fantasize about being the slave that they bought as the Boss, leaping up in the air to catch the football in the endzone. At that moment, we could be watching the science fiction movie Matrix where the human population is all in stasis, plugged into a life draining system that supports the fantasy of reality. But this is not the end of it.

The Alchemy of Money

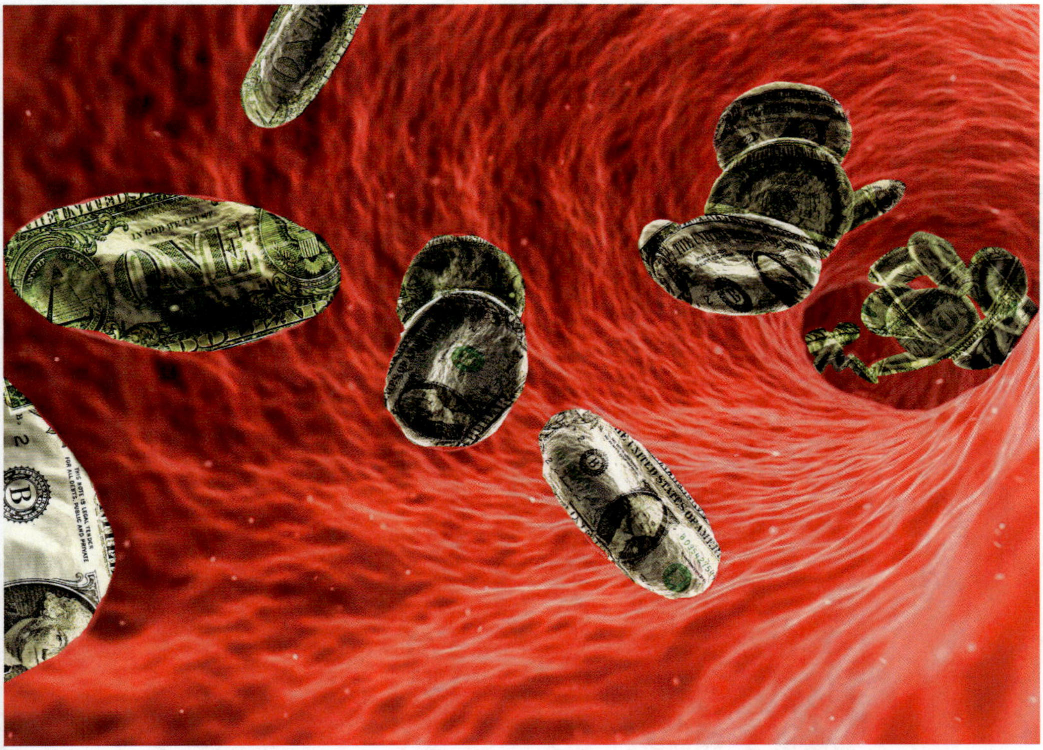

Illustration #18

Controlling the Flow of Blood

If conditioning and gate keeping are not enough, and the vampire capitalists are threatened by the government that they consider unfriendly to business, and the government seems reluctant to join in the feast and is bent on serving the people and the electorate that has elected them, the vampire capitalist can simply stop the flow of blood into the system and starve out the government through raising interest rates, refusing to invest, exporting money to foreign havens, moving production facilities abroad so as to effectively reduce demand and induce layoffs. A decline in demand triggers further cutbacks in investment and creates a downward spiral of recession that will be blamed on the reform government. But that is not the end.

When All Else Fails – The Final Solution and the Pact with the Devil

Capitalist would rather deal with dictators and Fascists and Nazis rather than socialist countries. This was the case before World War II when capitalists like the Bush family had no problem trading with Mussolini's Italy, Hitler's Germany, and Franco's Spain. The favoring of anti-democratic totalitarian governments versus truly democratic and socialist movements continues today in South America and other parts of the world. The fear of socialism comes from a deep fear by the capitalist class that their true nature will be revealed and that there is a hope of a brighter future with an alternative political and economic model that will nurture us all.

Illustration #19

Who Is in This Picture?

Albert Volger was a German industrialist. In 1912, he was Director of AG Iron and Steel Industries. In 1915, he was the head of German Luxembourg Mining. In 1925, he was the Chairman of Rhineland Westphalian Coal Syndicate, and in 1926, he became the head of the largest steel works in Germany. In 1928, he began funding the Nazi Party. He and other industrialists signed a letter urging Paul von Hindenburg to appoint Adolf Hitler as Chancellor of Germany, and prior to the March 1933 general election, Volger attended a meeting with Hitler at Herman Goring's home. At the meeting were the following industrialists and businessmen. (Volger)

1. Ernst Brandi - Chairman of *Bergbauverein*
2. Karl Büren - Director General of Braunkohlen- und Brikettindustrie AG, board member of *Deutschen Arbeitgeberverbände*
3. August Diehn - Board Member of Wintershall AG
4. Ludwig Grauert - Head of the Police Department of the Prussian Interior Ministry
5. Guenther Heubel - Director General of C. TH. Heye Braunkohlenwerke AG, board member of *Deutschen Arbeitgeberverbände*
6. Gustav Krupp von Bohlen und Halbachm – Head of Friedrick Krupp AG Hoeshch-Krupp
7. Hans von und zu Loewenstein - Executive Member of *Bergbauverein*
8. Fritz von Opel - Board Member of Adam Opel AG
9. Günther Quandt - Major Industrialist, later appointed Leader of the Armament Economy (*Wehrwirtschaftsführer*)
10. Wolfgang Reuter - Director General of Demag, chairman of *Vereins Deutscher Maschinenbau-Anstalten* - Presidential Member of *Reichsverbands der Deutschen Industrie*
11. August Rosterg - Director General of Wintershall AG
12. Hjalmar Schacht – President of Riechsbank Bank of Germany
13. Georg von Schnitzler - Board Member of IG Farben
14. Eduard Schulte - Director General of *Giesches Erben, Zink und Bergbaubetrieb*
15. Fritz Springorum - Hoesch AG
16. Hugo Stinnes Jr. - Board Member of *Reichsverband der Deutschen Industrie*, member of the Supervisory board of Rhenish-Westphalian Coal Syndicate
17. Ernst Tengelmann - CEO of Gelsenkirchener Bergwerks AG
18. **Albert Vögler, -** CEO of Vereinigte Stahlwerke AG
19. Ludwig von Winterfeld - Board Member of Siemens & Halske AG and Siemens-Schuckertwerke AG
20. Wolf-Dietrich von Witzleben - Head of the Office of Carl Friedrich von Siemens

> The group that night contributed $3 million marc (equivalent of approximately $40 million dollars in today's currency) to Hitler's election campaign, an election that ended all elections. In 1938 Volger joined the Nazi Party, and during the war he worked with Albert Spears as a Minister of Armaments. Volger committed suicide 14 April 1945 to avoid capture by the Allied troops. (Secret Meeting)

Theodor Adrian von Reneln was a German politician and activist. He headed the Hitler Youth then became a member of the Reichstag and led the Combat League of the Commercial Middle Class that participated in a boycott of Jewish businesses. He was then appointed President of the National Socialist Council of Industry and Trade and staff leader of the Labor Front and head of the Supreme Court of the Reich Labor Front. On July 1941, he was appointed the Generalkommissar of Generalbizirk Litauen (roughly modern Lithuania) where he ordered all telephones and lines to be stripped, postal services cut off, and bridges to the Kovno Ghetto to be surrounded by barbed wire fences to prevent Jews from jumping off the bridges. In 1943, he was implicated in the clearing of the Vilma Ghetto, deporting 20,000 Jews to concentration or death camps. It is believed that at the end of the war he was captured by the Russians and hanged. (Reneln)

Alfried Krupp von Bohlen und Halback was a German industrialist and a member of the Krupp family that had been prominent German industrialist since the 18th century. The family company Friedrick Krupp AG Hoesch-Krupp was a key supplier of weapons and war materials for the Nazi regime. Krupp's father Gustave was at the 1933 meeting with Volger, and like his father, Afried in his pursuit of profit saw the advantage of supporting the Nazi's, their militarism, and their opposition to independent labor unions. He joined he Nazi Party in 1938, and he was a supporting member of the SS. During the war he was appointed Minister of Armament and War Production, and the company thrived through its weapons and munition sales, the acquiring of factories in occupied Europe, and the transfer of factory-machinery and materials from the occupied territories to Germany.

After the war, he was prosecuted and found guilty of using slave and forced labor on a massive scale during the war. It was estimated the 23,000 prisoners of war and 70,000 forced slave laborers worked in the Krupp factories under conditions of severely inadequate food rations, clothing, and housing. Eastern European and Russian prisoners of war and forced slave laborers were treated the worse. It is estimated that only 43% of the Russian prisoners of war survived, and Eastern European women were forced to work a mandatory 56-69 hours a week under the most squalid conditions. Krupp also employed 5,000 Jewish concentration camp prisoners. He was even charged with planning a weapons factory at Auschwitz prison camp where Jews were being gassed to death. At the war crimes trials, Krupp was sentenced to twelve years in prison, paroled in three, and his property was returned to him.

> The Leviathan that Afried Krupp created survived. For the rest of the 20th century, the company was an important manufacturer of industrial machinery and materials. It became a limited liability company in 1968 when its assets were transferred from the private ownership of the Krupp family to the Krupp Foundation. It then merged with Thyssen to become Thyssen Krupp a leading global manufacturer of steel, construction material, automotive part and assemblies, and industrial mechanical services. It should be noted that Fritz Thyssen, the creator of Thyssen Industries was a steel magnate who joined the Nazi movement in the early 1920s and was famous for his book, *I Was Paid by Hitler*. (Krupp) (Krupp Wikipedia)

The fact that these Leviathans created by these two men in the cradle of the Nazi Regime are alive and well today, transcending their founders with a life of their own, conjures up our nightmares filtered through the horror movies that we watch, the many science fiction movies where the machines take over and turn us all into slave labor or find it more cost efficient to exterminate us all. These horror stories hide the truth of the real monsters that are alive today, but it doesn't end here, and the question becomes, can it happen here?

New York Ti

Copyright, 1934, by The New York Times Company.

NEW YORK, WEDNESDAY, NOVEMBER 21, 1934.

P ISSUE
STRIKE
TRATION

to Submit

Gen. Butler Bares 'Fascist Plot' To Seize Government by Force

Says Bond Salesman, as Representative of Wall St. Group, Asked Him to Lead Army of 500,000 in March on Capital—Principals in Angry Denials—Dickstein Gets Charge.

A plot of Wall Street interests to overthrow President Roosevelt and ... dictatorship,

Thomas W. Lamont, partner in the firm of J. P. Morgan & Co., said:

"Perfect moonshine! Too unut- ... to comment

ROOS
GO
R

Clo

Illustration #20

Can It Happen Here?

With the Great Depression and the election of FDR, the vampire capitalists were experiencing a serious threat to their control of the flow of blood through the body politic and the way it would be distributed. FDR was in the process of creating socialist overlay to an essentially capitalist system to ameliorate its excesses, and it was affecting the vampire capitalist's bottom line. For example, FDR took America off the gold standard, a move that the monied interests felt would induce an inflation and threaten the value of their money and the money owed to them. They felt it was a plot to redistribute wealth. They were also vehemently against (1) the regulation of the banking system, i.e. reforms like the Glass Seagall Act that separated investment banks from commercial saving and loan banks. (2) the creation of the Security and Exchange Commission that would regulate trade in stocks and bonds and punish inside trading etc. (3) the Commodities Trade Commission that regulated speculation in commodities, and (4) the New Deal's attempt to strengthen independent unions and implement a progressive income taxes.

Special Council Ferdinand Pecora, a former district attorney from New York, was appointed by FDR to the Banking Commission to investigate Wall Street. In *Wall Street Under Oath*, a book that he wrote about the vampire capitalists that controlled the flow of blood through the body politic, he said, "Undoubtedly, this small group of highly placed financiers, controlling the springs of economic activity, hold more real power than any similar group in the United States." (Duff 9-10) An example that Pecora used in his book is the House of J.P Morgan. He describes it as a great stream that is fed by many sources, by its deposits, by its loans, by its promotions, by its directorships that controlled 169 industries, banks, railroads, and utilities, by its preeminent position as an investment banker, by its control of holdings companies which, in turn, control scores of subsidiaries, and by its silken bonds of gratitude in which it skillfully enmeshes the chosen ranks of the preferred list and friends of the bank who are let into a market at below-market prices. In Pecora's investigation of J.P. Morgan, what was probably most shocking to the American public was that J.P. Morgan, who was probably the most powerful banker in American, paid no income tax in 1931 and 1932. (Duff 11)

Many bankers, industrialist, and businessmen saw the New Deal as a threat to their privileged position within American society, and many voiced their disapproval and praised Nazi Germany and Fascist Italy as viable alternatives. For example, as early as 1923 the American Legion voiced its affinity to fascism when the Legion's Commander in Chief, Alvin Owley, was quoted as saying, "If ever needed, the American Legion stands ready to protect our country's institutions and ideals as the Fascisti dealt with the destructionists who menaced Italy." Asked if this meant taking over the government, he stated, "exactly that... Do not forget that the Fascisti are to Italy what the American Legion is to the United States." (Duff 13-14)

In July 1934 Henry Luce's Fortune magazine devoted an entire issue to Mussolini. In the article we're told that "Fascism is achieving in a few years or decades such a conquest of the spirit of man as Christianity achieved only in centuries, and the good journalist must recognize in Fascism certain ancient virtues of the race, whether or not they happen to be momentarily fashionable in his own country. Among these are Discipline, Duty, Courage, Glory, and Sacrifice."(Duff 22) David Reed, a United States Senator from

Pennsylvania in May 1932, said on the floor of the Senate, "I do not envy other countries and their government, but I say that if this country ever needed a Mussolini, it needs one now."(Duff 29)

Illustration #21

It was during this era of discontent that Gerald C. MacGuire approached Marine Corp Major General Smedley Darlington Butler, America's then most decorated officer who had won two Congressional Medals of Honor. MacGuire was an employee of Colonel Grayson Mollet-Provost Murphy, and he ran a leading New York brokerage that, working with J.P. Morgan, traded in stocks and international bond syndicates. Grayson Murphy, who was on Morgan's "preferred client list," was a director of Morgan's Guarantee Trust bank and several Morgan-connected corporations. He and his banking house had played an important role in syndicating Morgan loans to Fascist Italy for which he was decorated by Mussolini.

> Butler was very popular with the veterans and spent a great deal of time going to veteran organizations like the VFW and speaking to the members about issues that were important to

> them like the bonus payment that they were demanding from the government. At the first meeting, MacGuire wanted Butler to go around to veteran organizations and talk about the return to the gold standard. Butler refused, and the second time that MacGuire met with Butler he came with Robert S. Baker, a member of Morgan's preferred client list and the heir to the Singer Sewing Machine fortune. Clark attempted to bribe Butler, but Butler refused once again to participate in the plan to promote the return to the gold standard. At the third meeting, McGuire revealed a plan to take over the government. Butler was to organize a 500,000 man army drawing from the veteran organizations and the new Liberty League that was being formed for exactly this purpose by an executive committee consisting of the Morgan lawyer John W Davis, the former democratic presidential candidate; Irenee du Pont, who ran the duPont fortune; Nathan Miller, the former GOP Governor of New York; Representative James Wadsworth (R-NY), a supporter of the gold standard; and Al Smith who ran for president against FDR. (Duff 25)
>
> The plan was for General Butler to lead a 500,000 men army and march on Washington. They were to demand that FDR appoint General Butler to a new cabinet post that would in reality make Butler the head of the government, and FDR would remain the figure head, much like the King of Italy was in Fascist Italy where Mussolini ruled as a dictator. MacGuire assured Butler that a consortium of leading industrialists, bankers, and businessmen were behind the plot to take over the government, and that all the money that he would need was available to him. (Duff 24)

General Butler informed Tom O'Neill, the city editor of the Philadelphia Record of this plot, and O'Neil had one of his reporters, Paul Comley French, pose as an intermediator between Butler and MacGuire to negotiate the deal. French confirmed everything that Butler had claimed, and, in addition, he was offered $1 million dollars out front to get the operation moving. MacGuire also told French there would be no problem getting weapons for Butler's army from the duPont controlled Remington Arms Company.

Before Butler, French, and O'Neil could go public with the plot, investigators from the Special House Committee to Investigate Nazi Activities in the United States got wind of it, and they arranged to have General Butler testify behind closed doors to the Committee. Both MacGuire and French were called to testify, and the investigators uncovered letters from McGuire to John Davis, the Morgan lawyer on the executive board of the Liberty League that substantiated much of what Butler claimed. At the end of the hearing, the Committee released the following statement.

> *"In the last few weeks of the committee's official life, it received evidence that certain persons had tried to establish a fascist organization in our country. No evidence was presented, and this committee had none to show a connection between this effort and any fascist activity of any European country. There is no question that these attempts were discussed, were planned, and might have been placed in execution when and if the financial backers deemed expedient...*
>
> *The committee received evidence from Major General Smedley D. Butler (ret.) twice decorated by the Congress of the United States. He testified before the committee on conversations with one Gerald C. MacGuire in which the latter is alleged to have suggested the formation of a fascist army under the leadership of General Butler.*
>
> *McGuire denied these allegations under oath, but our committee was able to verify all the pertinent statements of General Butler, except for the direct statement suggesting the creation of the organization. This however was corroborated in the correspondence of MacGuire...while MacGuire was abroad studying various forms of organizations of fascist character. 1(Duff 33)*

That was it. The Commission never disclosed the full transcript of the testimony or the hearing to the public or followed up with an investigation of the prominent bankers and businessmen implicated in the planning and support of the conspiracy. The corporate press ridiculed the story or did not cover it, and it was soon buried. But is that the end of it?

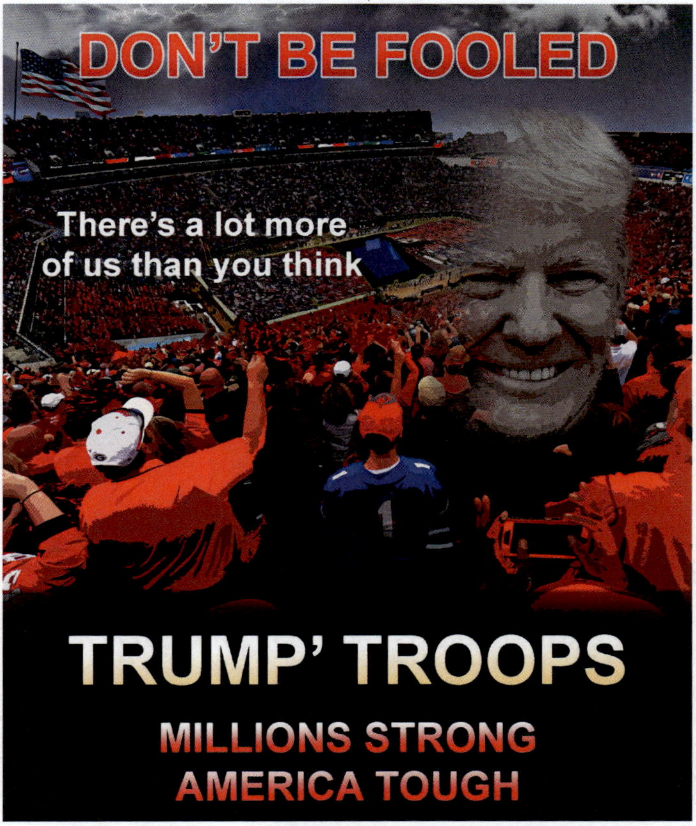

Illustration #22

Is It Happening Now?

Is this it? Is this what it has all come to? Is Trump the monster child of vampire capitalism? Is he the harbinger of the rise of Fascism in America? Why have the reforms to capitalism failed?

The New Deal and The Welfare State

As noted earlier in the study, the New Deal and the Welfare State turned out to be only a Band-aid that at its best merely ameliorated the excesses of capitalism, but now we see a roll back of all the New Deal reforms and the rise of the corporate state and global corporate feudalism. You could say that vampire capitalism was only in remission, but the cancer is growing again. Why? Because capitalism remained at the core of our system, and it had to grow again.

The Welfare State tried to guarantee certain rights and freedoms from the abuses of capitalism and at the same guarantee the right to a better life in the pursuit of happiness, but it failed to control capitalism and failed in its promises primarily because it failed to give us, the American people, the power to decide for ourselves, the power to insure those rights and freedom, and secure for ourselves that promise for a better life. In some ways the conservative criticism of the Welfare State is right, it does create a passive dependency on the state to secure those rights and freedoms when we should be making those decisions for ourselves and taking on the responsibilities of truly sovereign people in a direct and participatory political and economic democracy.

Giving Us a Taste – ESOPs and Pension Plans

More recently, the vampire capitalists have tried to reform the system and maintain their dominance by giving everyone a taste and thereby make them feel like they are in on the feast. One of the ways this is done is through Employee Stock Ownership Plans and Pension Plans. In the case of ESOPs, we must distinguish between appearances and reality. In the United States there are 7000 firms covering 10 million employees that are estimated as having some degree of employee ownership.

> However, there are only several hundred firms where the employees own a majority of the stock and very few instances where they have the power to make decisions that owners would make in their own interest. (Bachrach 104-105) In fact, a participation project at Polaroid was stopped according to a Polaroid official because it was too successful. “What were we going to do with the supervisors and managers? We didn’t need them anymore.” The whole idea was too much of a threat to the very meaning of their lives and the management myth. (Bachrach 103-104)

Another way in which the vampire capitalists make us feel like we are in on the feast is through our pension funds, but that is a myth too. In reality, fewer and fewer Americans have pension funds, and for those of us that have, whatever gains we receive are miniscule compared to what we lose in increased hours of work for less pay and excessive costs for health care and education. In fact, the profits from the pension plans do not go to the workers. They go to the wealthiest 10% who hold 62% of all the value of pension accounts and most of the remainder goes to the financial institutions that administer the account. Quite simply, you are tasting your own blood, and they take out more than they put back in.

The system is far more beneficial to the upper middle class, the professional classes and pundits that serve their masters with useful expertise, i.e. the junior or contingent members of the vampire class who are part of the 20% of the population that control 80% of the wealth and income in America, the classes we referred to earlier in our pyramid diagram of the Aztec temple of trickledown economics. This class of professions can significantly enhance their income by feeding off the collective blood bank with safe "investments" in the stock market. This taste will not only make them dependent and well fed, but it will also link them to the system through shared guilt. For the rest of us, we are tasting our own blood and cannibalizing ourselves.

European Social Democracies

For many years, the social democracies of Europe have fared far better than the United States in protecting its citizens from the abuses of capitalism. They accomplished this with a far more embracing view of the Welfare State and the rights and freedoms of their citizens, or, in other words, the life blood of the society flowed more equitably through the body politic, and the money spent as nourishment to each and every body cell manifests itself through the alchemy of money into universal health care, affordable education and vocational training, strong independent unions and labor laws, and far more services and support for the unemployed, the impoverished and the aged than in the United States.

> Based upon the 17 sustainability goals for peace and prosperity for the people and the planet established by the UN in 2015, using the data from the blueprint of the 2016 report by the Organization of Economic Cooperation and Development (OECD), the United States scored far below Europe in quality of life and barely looked like a developed country. (Merelli)

However, like the United States, Europe has made the same mistake that the US made during the New Deal era. Despite all the reforms, capitalism remained at the heart of the economic system. Like the Americans, they believed they could control something that has to grow, or it will die; and now, it is a full-blown cancer in Europe. The corporate and financial global Leviathans of Europe have taken control of the EU. They have implemented free market capitalism so that they can control the flow of blood, and they have opened the borders to bare the necks of the host nations and weaken their sovereign power. Like the United States, Europe is seeing the rise of right-wing populist parties and organizations in response to the inability of their government to protect their rights and freedoms and defend them against capitalist abuses. Basically, they are making the same mistake that we made. We and they have focused too much on rights and freedoms and not enough on direct participation by the people in the political and economic decision-making process. However, there are two important examples in Europe of the participation of labor in economic decision making and employee ownership of the means of production that we need to study for their strengths and weaknesses.

Codetermination

There are two boards in the German system of codetermination, the supervisory board and the management board. The management board is elected by the supervisory board and consists of the executives that manage the day to day operations of the corporation. On that board is also one elected member from labor who oversees Human Resources. The Supervisory Board for companies with 500-2000 employees consists of $1/3^{rd}$ the board being represented by labor, and companies with 2000 and over employees consists of equal members of worker elected representatives and shareholder elected representatives with the head of the board being elected by the shareholders. The Supervisory Board members are jointly responsible for monitoring firm operations, the appointment and dismissal of CEOs, the management and crafting of strategic and tactical investment direction, holding management accountable to the board, and the ethical and legal structure established for the business. The other important feature of the codetermination model is the worker's council, an employee/management bodies that meet regularly and determines policy on med-level management issues like scheduling and workplace changes.

Has codetermination been successful? Codetermination in one form or another has been in place since the 1950s, and if it wasn't successful and efficient and added value to the company and the workplace, it would have been abandoned decades ago. Instead, it has spread from Germany to 2/3rd of the EU, and it has resulted in long term planning and investment, higher wages, the expansion of the high skill labor sector, a shorter work week, more expenditures on research and technology, and community responsibility. The Bertelsmann Foundation's 2018 global assessment concluded that the five highest quality democracies were all countries that have all implemented codetermination as an intricate part of their economy. It's panel of international political scientists judged the quality of American democracy, i.e. how well citizen voices and sentiments are reflected in public policy, and the US ranked only 18th. Separately, the Freedom House annual international update on the global state of Liberty found that freedom and political rights were also stronger in each of the major adopters of codetermination than they were in the US. (Tyler)

However, the fact that the head of the board is selected by the shareholders and possesses the deciding vote between labor and ownership, causes codetermination in Germany to remain capitalistic at its core. This is ameliorated somewhat by the worker councils where workers have an equal voice with management on a wide range of matters including job evaluation, working hours and overtime, social and welfare provisions in case of mass layoffs, training, accident prevention, and worker conduct on the plant floor. However, in many instances, it is the union leadership that dominates the decision process, and the union leadership tends on the highest levels to distance themselves from the workers on the floor and identify more with the people that they work with day to day – management.

Although there are significant differences in form between German codetermination schemes and the Swedish system of collective bargaining, the outcomes of the two systems seem strikingly similar. Both systems have transformed the balance of power within the firms in favor of unions, but they have nevertheless preserved the fundamentally capitalist nature of management, and in neither system have the workers themselves, as opposed to their union representatives gained a meaningful voice in determining the policies of the firm.

Though the codetermination model is superior to anything we have in the United States as a model for worker and corporate relations, the codetermination model has several flaws. As noted, the labor segment of the relationship is dominated by union organizations that are not democratic in their decision processes, and their leadership tend to identify with the corporate leadership that they work with day to day. As the workers on the floor would say, "They're the suits." Another flaw is that there is no public input to ensure that the corporation is serving the common good. Finally, and most importantly, because the head of the board is selected by the stockholders, the corporation remains at its core, capitalistic, and, therefore, vulnerable to the free market neo-liberal economic ideology that is virulent in Germany and the EU today. In fact, there are several legal cases in the EU courts that have questioned the compatibility of codetermination with EU law. In interesting question in relationship to EU law and what German can do and can't do as a sovereign nation is, what would happen if the voters in Germany changed the codetermination laws and stipulated that the head of the board of directors had to be elected by all representatives on the board and not just the stockholders? The answer to this question may be found in the French effort to nationalize important segments of their economy in an effort to reform capitalism and create a hybrid of socialism and capitalism, and what happens when the vampire capitalist think that the government has gone too far.

Nationalization in France

After World War Two, France was in ruins, and the post-war government of Charles De Gaulle nationalized critical sectors of the economy as part of a massive effort to reconstruct their economy. Through the efforts of a leader that many believed to be a conservative right-wing President, De Gaulle transformed the government into a major economic player in the French economy.

> The French government controlled 98% of coal production, 75% of electricity, 58% of the banking sector, 38% of the automobile production, and 15% of the total GDP. (Cohen)

France through its economic reconstruction effort enjoyed over thirty years of growth and prosperity. From 1950 to the 1970s, France's GDP grew

5% per year while during the same period, in one of the more prosperous eras in American economic history, GNP in the United States grew 3.6% per year. (Cohen) At the same time, unemployment in France was near zero and working-class men and women saw dramatic increases in their standard of living, but like the United States, the 70s brought globalization, stagflation, the exporting of their industrial base, and competition with cheap slave and child labor in countries with no environmental or labor regulations.

Conservative governments that came into power during this era began a process of privatizing the nationalized industries. The priests of neo-liberal capitalism preached open borders, a common currency for Europe, and a united economic system based on free market capitalism. In response to this right-wing surge and the fact that France had lost 700,000 jobs in the industrial sector during this period and the standard of living for your average French citizen was in decline, the socialist Francois Mitterrand was elected President of France in 1981, and he immediately moved forward on his campaign promises to nationalize seven key industries along with thirty-six banks. At the same time, he implemented Keynesian type economic policies of government spending and investment so as to stimulate the economy, create jobs, and put money into the hands of consumers through increasing government employment, raising the minimum wage, a guaranteed income for retirees, and the increased productivity that would cause the revitalization of its industrial base and the stabilizing of the banking industry. He planned to pay for these expenditures by increasing the inheritance tax and increasing the tax on the wealthy.

The response of the inheritors, the wealthy, and the vampires who controlled the blood banks in France, Europe, and the rest of the capitalist world was to turn off the flow of blood to the French economy, and that was it. The Bank of France raised interest rates causing the value of the French currency to raise. This hard money policy negatively affected industries that depended on low interest rates, i.e. consumers, the auto industry, construction, exports, etc. In addition, domestic and foreign financial institutions and businesses cut off investments in the French economy, laid off workers, and exported their money to foreign havens and investments outside of France. At the same time, the blood banks were making more money off money because the price of blood went up.

The French economy tanked, and the public blamed the Mitterrand government for the economic collapse. Mitterrand and his administration were at the mercy of the bankers, and in order for the economy to be bailed out by the vampire capitalists that caused the collapse, Mitterrand had to throw himself and his administration and all the reforms to capitalism that they had implemented on the Aztec alter of human sacrifice and watch, still alive and pulsing, the heart of his reforms being torn out as he was forced to implement an austerity program, reduce government spending, roll back the welfare state and government investment in the economy, and move forward in the trans-European negotiations that resulted in the 1992 Treaty of Maastricht, the creation of the European monetary union, in imposition of open borders and free market rules, and the subsequent EU treaties that committed member states to privatization.

The question now becomes, how efficient were the nationalized industries and how efficient are they today in France, and to what extent have they served the common good? Neo-liberal economists and pundits would like us to believe that the French nationalization program was a total failure. High priests of free market capitalism, like Milton Friedman, ridiculed Mitterrand's plan, and at the same time, encouraged the head the United States Federal Reserve, Paul Volcker, to increase interest rates over and over again to combat stagflation, a policy that tanked the American economy in the same way that it tanked the French economy. It was this policy of hard money that enabled the Japanese to penetrate the American market with lower priced cars simply based on currency exchange and the value of the dollar versus the yen. Hard money affected the price of all exports, and the high interest rates effected consumer credit and all industries that relied on low interest rates, i.e. the building and construction industry. As noted earlier, the only winners were the banks, financial institutions, credit card companies, bond holders, and the possessors of money.

The facts do not support the perceptions of the free market faithful. Among the six largest industrial groups nationalized in France in 1982, several of which were losing money and going under, all six were turning a profit in 1985, and at the same time, the employees were experiencing more job security, better pay, and better working conditions. (Cohen) From a perspective other than efficiency, the significance of government ownership and its prime objective of serving the public good over profit was highlighted in the government's takeover of the coal industry. The coal industry and mining was being phased out for both economic and environmental reasons, but unlike Thatcher's United Kingdom where miners and workers in the coal industry were essentially thrown out onto the street to fend for themselves, the Mitterrand government initiated a decade long plan to wind down the industry and gradually displaced the workers through retirement and placement in other government owned industries. The government also saved jobs in a steel industry that was on the brink of bankruptcy. The steel industries that the government owned were streamlined so as to compete in the contemporary global market, and by 1990 France was the second leading producer of steel in the world, and though they still struggle to keep out of the red, the French steel industry never suffered what we have seen in the United States where large segments of America that relied on steel production have turned into a rust belt of unemployment, poverty, and abandonment.

> The Mitterrand government also invested in technology and new industries. An example of this was the revitalization of Air France and the investment in the British-French-German Air Bus Consortium. The French government still owns 13% of the company that reported $2 billion dollars in profits in 2008. Even today after years of conservative government and the EU trying to privatize the European economies, a significant share of the French economy still is in the government's hands. In 2006, the state controlled 90 companies directly and 755 companies indirectly, and in 2007, the portfolios of these companies were estimated at $191.9 billion euros. (Cohen)

The neo-liberal pundits and believers in free market capitalism like to point out the failures of the French government's nationalization of key industries, i.e. Credit Lyonnais and Elf-Aquitaine, but the privatized sector has its failures too, and the failures of the French government does not compare to the failures in the United States, i.e. Enron, General Motors, the Savings and Loan collapse and scandals, and the 2008 collapse of the mortgage markets and the private financial sectors in United States.

From our point of view, however, France's attempts to reform capitalism through the nationalization of key industries and services and creating a hybrid of capitalism and socialism had significant and critical flaws. The most important of these flaws is the fact that they left capitalism intact to fester at the core of the economy. When threatened, it was able to reverse all the efforts to reform it by simply cutting off the flow of blood to the body politic. Also, the government reforms, for the most part, were for the people, not by the people as it should be in a truly democratic economy where the employees directly share in the ownership of the enterprise and directly participate in the decision making processes. However, there is in Europe an important example of a successful large-scale cooperative network that is owned and managed by its employees and is much closer to the concept of true economic democracy than the codetermination model.

The Mondragon Cooperative Network

The Mondragon cooperative network, located in the Basque region of Spain, is the largest business group in the region, and the 7th largest in all of Spain. It includes more than 150 cooperative enterprises with 60,000 workers, and it has over 8 billion euros in working capital. It is the largest and most successful example of worker-owned industrial cooperatives in the world. Compared to capitalist firms, the Mondragon cooperative provides greater opportunities for workers to participate in decision making and enjoys a more equitable pay structure. Compared to other cooperatives, the Mondragon support network is far more robust and developed, especially the cooperative bank that provides cooperatives in the network with extensive research assistance on technology, products, markets, in-depth training in cooperative principles of management, substantial financial support, and an entrepreneurial division that researches new production and marketing possibilities and encourages the set-up of new cooperatives. Mondragon, in addition, has created a network of educational institutions to train its employees and provide a quality education for the children of its employees. For example, Escuela Politecnica, a college created by and financed by the Mondragon Cooperative Network, offers an education comparable to three years of the four-year undergraduate programs in the United States. Within their educational network they offer degrees that will directly benefit the cooperative network, i.e. business and engineering degrees, post graduate program where the students work with the coops in developing new products, advanced school of industrial design, and a school that provides intensive instruction in English, French, German, and the Basque Language of Euskera.

The Mondragon Cooperatives Network is managed by a President and his General Council which is comprised of nine vice-presidents (one per group or division) and the directors of the six Mondragon Central Departments. The management bodies are accountable to two representative bodies, the Cooperative Congress and a Cooperative Standing Committee. The Cooperative Congress is made up of representatives elected from all the cooperatives in the Corporation (in indirect proportion to their size) and is the basic policy-making body for Mondragon as a whole. The Standing Committee consists of 17 people elected from the Cooperative Congress. The Standing Committee appoints the President of the Mondragon Cooperative Network (the CEO), and they must approve the President's choices for the General Council. Basically, the Standing Committee generally serves as an internal board of director.

However, the Mondragon Cooperative Network does have some flaws in its organization. Over the years there has been an unmistakable drift towards greater managerial domination of decision making, and though Mondragon maintains a representative democratic process, de-facto power has become increasingly centralized in the hands of technocratic business managers who manage the cooperative's money. There is also a significant trend towards greater wage disparities within the cooperative, and Mondragon vested members increasingly stand out as a privileged sector in the regional work force. Also, while Mondragon cooperatives are more responsive to community needs than their capitalist counterparts, when profits conflict with community interests, Mondragon's cooperatives increasingly favor money over public interest and the commonwealth of their community, region, and nation. Also, today well over half the capital of their cooperative bank is invested in non-cooperative ventures, and many Mondragon cooperatives have entered in partnership with multinational corporations and opened non-cooperative factories in Third World countries.

Where do we go from here? We revealed the horror story behind the labyrinth of lies that hide the truth. Vampire capitalism is real, and it is a cancerous growth that in the end will kill us all and consume the planet if we don't come up with an alternative vision. In Part One of The New American Revolution we revealed our political revolution, a political democracy where we the people of the United States directly participate in our government through the initiative, referendum, and recall process at every level of government. Direct and participatory democracy becomes the University of Our Lives where with every vote, every debate, every decision, and every issue we grow, we learn to come together, and we make decisions on those issues and policies that affect all our lives. We see the world from all our points of view, from all our experiences, and we create a collective mind that reflects each and every one of our unique points of view. That is the goal, but we are only halfway there because when we go to work, we live most of our waking hours in an authoritarian state called our job.

> We have looked at the traditional attempt to reform capitalism, but as we have noted, all the attempts at reform that we surveyed have flaws that have pretty much left us where we started from, with a fatal disease. Part Two of the New American Revolution is an alternative that finally banishes vampire capitalism by revealing its true image and destroying the cancer at the heart of our system and replacing it with an economic system that does not suck the life blood out of each and every one of us but nourishes us all and democratizes our economy so that it is an economy of, by and for the people. Essentially, we are turning capitalism on its head.

PART FIVE: Economic Democracy by the People

Illustration #23

An Economy of the People, by the People, and for the People

How are we going to free ourselves of the horror stories that are real, the vampires, the Leviathans, the aliens that emerge from blood pods to use us as larva wombs for a new generation of aliens that bleed and drool an acid that eats away at anything that it touches. How are we going to free ourselves from a horror stories that is so real, so inhuman that we need to imagine it as an alien invasion? How are we going to vanquish these monsters that are so rich, so vast, so far way? Individually, we are defenseless, and that is the way they like to keep us, divided by class, race, gender, ethnic origins, and all the other ways they fragment us and hide the simple truth, and that is, We the People of the United States own this country. Together, you and me, all of us collectively are the sovereign kings of the richest most powerful economy in the world with a Gross National Product of 1932 billion dollars and asset valued at 225 trillion dollars.

We rule here.

> This should be the battle cry of the new American revolution. We need to take back our country, not only politically but also economically by going into partnership with the workers of America, which is to say that we are going into business with ourselves. We will all become entrepreneurs in a system where inspiration and new ideas and the potential for leadership circulates through the whole body politic and can be found everywhere and anywhere with the means to implement our hopes and dream for our economy into reality.

Any or all of our goals for our economy can originate at any and all levels of government, (1) by citizen initiatives (2) by referendums (3) by entrepreneurs or groups of entrepreneurs and workers proposing new businesses directly to planning boards or to the people directly through the initiative process. (4) by recommendations and proposals from research centers and by research centers that are networked with the planning boards, legislatures, and the businesses that are part of our network of economic democracies. Through this system of direct economic democracy we will create new enterprises, industries, and services, restore and revitalize the old, produce new products, create new technologies, and invest in pure science and research that will open new horizons of discovery. Quite simply, we are going to make life better for everyone.

In the workplace democracies that we will be creating, the citizen investors will elect half the members of the board of directors of the businesses that they create and the workers will elect the other half of the board. Collectively, the workers and the citizen investors will elect the CEO and the head of the board of directors, and the CEO will select their management staff with the approval of the board. The CEO, board of directors the management staff, and the workers in cooperation and coordination with one another are responsible for the organization of the workplace, discipline, hiring and firing policies, what to produce, how to produce it, where and how much to produce, and the salaries to be paid. The workers and the citizen investors not only elect their representatives to the board of directors, they also participate directly in the management of the enterprise through the instrumentality of the initiative, referendum, and recall processes where they can initiate, challenge and reverse decisions made by the CEO and the board of directors. They also have the power through the recall process to remove the CEO, any member of the board of directors and the management staff. At quarterly intervals, a general assembly will be called where the workers, the board of directors, the CEO, the management staff, and citizen investors can meet, discuss and debate issues, present propositions as initiatives by the workers or citizen investors or referendums by the CEO, and/or the board, the management staff, and the legislature. The meetings will be open to the public, and broadcasted through a nationwide communications network called, *The People's Business*.

So, what do we do about the profits? The citizen investors and the workers share equally in the net profit after the cost of salaries, operational expenses, liabilities, and investment in new products, services, and research, etc. are deducted. This is an important point. The citizen's share of the profits does not go to government, they go directly into the citizen's individual investment account. Or, in other words,

We Get the Money!

Illustration #24

Economic Democracy and the Private Sector

The first stage of the democratization of the private sector will be the implementation of codetermination. Similarly, to codetermination in Germany, corporations that employ over 2000 employees will be converted to corporations where half the board of directors is represented by labor and the other half by stockholders. However, unlike German codetermination, the head of the board of directors will not be selected by the stockholders. He or she will be elected by the board of directors. The members of the board and the CEO are jointly responsible for monitoring firm operations, the crafting of strategic and tactical investments direction, holding management accountable to the board, and the ethical and legal structure established for the business. Like German codetermination, a worker's council will meet with mid-level management regularly on issues like job evaluation, social and welfare provisions in case of mass layoffs, training, working conditions, worker's health and safety, scheduling, and worker conduct on the job. As noted with Germany, codetermination, has resulted in more long-term planning, investment, higher wages, expansion of the high skilled labor sector, shorter work week, more expenditures on research and technology, and community responsibility. Unlike German codetermination, where the head of the board is elected by the stockholders, the head of the board in our system will be elected by a board where the workers are equally represented. Through this system the workers will not only have all the advantages of German codetermination, but they will also have more input into the management and policy decisions of the corporation, greater protection against hostile takeovers, and a more equitable share in the profits.

Because of the magnitude of the task, the phase two breakup of the private sector Leviathans will have to be done in stages. On the top of our list of conglomerates that will need to be broken up and democratized are the media giants. These Leviathans cannot be allowed to control information, communications, and our dream world. We can't allow the vampire capitalists who control these monsters to determine what we hear and see. We can't allow them, in the name of profit, to turn every value that we cherish into a commodity to be bought and sold, or as Michael Eisner, the CEO of Walt Disney Co. says in defense of capitalism, "We have no obligation to make history. We have no obligation to make art. We have no obligation to make a statement. To make money is our only objective." Or as Robert W. McChesney wrote in *The New Global Media; It's a Small World of Big Conglomerates*,

> "Global conglomerates can at times have a progressive impact on culture, especially when they enter nations that had been tightly controlled by corrupt crony media systems (as in much of Latin America) or nations that had significant state censorship over media (as in parts of Asia). The global commercial-media system is radical in that it will respect no tradition or custom, on balance, if it stands in the way of profits. But ultimately it is politically conservative, because the media giants are significant beneficiaries of the current social structure around the world, and any upheaval in property or social relations - particularly to the extent that it reduces the power of business -is not in their interest. (McChesney)

We need to break up these conglomerates and their branding of America. We need to transform them into true economic democracies. Therefore, unlike phase one where we implemented codetermination, the stockholders in phase two will be bought out and issued non-voting bonds equivalent to the value of the stock. The bonds will pay out at an acceptable interest rate by government bond standards until the original value of the bond is bought off. In the companies that are created by the breakup of these monsters, the employees will elect half the members of the board of directors and the citizen investors will elect the other half with the CEO and the head of the board of directors being elected by the board. The CEO will select their management staff with the approval of the board, and the workers and the citizen investors will directly participate in the management of the firm through the instrumentality of the initiative, referendum, and recall process.

> The primary fear about who controls the mass media and our news networks is that either the government or, conversely, a dominate and powerful private interest group will control the media. In our system the media will reflect a broad-based representation of workers (which includes the profession journalist, producers, creative personnel, the management staff, the CEO, and the custodian, as well as the citizen consumers and citizen investors. In a workplace democracy all our civil liberties are alive and well here, including freedom of speech.

The Flow of Blood That Nurtures All

In the economy of the People, by the People, and for the People, we are going to eliminate the Federal Reserve System that only serves the rich. We will replace it with a nationalized and democratized banking system in which the blood will flow through the body politic and nourish all the body parts, all the cells and selves, each and every one of us. It will be an interest free banking system, and with the elimination of compound interest, we will surgically remove one of the main causes of the cancerous growth of capitalism and its need to continually grow, maximize profit, and spread throughout the globe.

The money that flows through the system will flow on a per capita basis to every region and locality in the country except for priority projects that will be determined democratically. An example of a priority project is a national plan to coordinate the transportation and energy industries and services so as to create a sustainable transportation and energy system that is totally devoid of dependency on fossil fuels and runs on renewable energy sources that will not pollute the environment. Another example of a priority program would be to direct investment and resources into areas that would be affected negatively by the transformation from fossil fuels to renewable energy source, i.e. the coal regions of America that would need to be nourished so as to relieve the workers of an economic burden of a transformation that will benefit us all. This can be done through immediate financial relieve, retraining, and the creation of new industries where we the people will go into partnership with the displaced worker and create a new economy.

In this system of economic democracy where the blood flows equitably on a per capita bases, we can expect national development to be more balanced. Communities will be more stable, and there will be more opportunities for our children to stay home and work where they live, and we will be more willing to invest in our community as a way of life. Also, as noted, through our system, we are more able to coordinate our efforts nationally and pour blood into projects that will save us all and come to the aid of fellow citizens and areas of our country in need of restoration and revival. We can do this because we are creating an economic and banking system that is an organic whole, and when you stick a pin anywhere in the system, we will all go, "Ouch."

Entrepreneurship

Too often capitalists like to convince us that capitalism and entrepreneurship are one and the same, but they are not. Too often capitalists like to justify capitalism by pointing out the virtues of entrepreneurship, but entrepreneurship can exist and thrive without capitalism, and they are not irretrievably linked. Even neoliberal free market economists will agree that they are distinct functions. To make the distinction clear, a capitalist is someone who makes money off of money, whereas an entrepreneur is someone who brings together (1) the creative vision of a new business, (2) the resources, i.e. physical assets such as land, machinery, etc. (3) the labor and specific skills relevant to the business. (4) and the necessary capital funding.

In our system of economic democracy, individual genius and creativity are nurtured, valued, and rewarded. Entrepreneurs have a multiplicity of opportunities to create a startup in our system of economic democracy where the American people are the venture capitalists who have turned capitalism on its head and capitalized themselves so as to serve everyone's interests in an interest free economy. An entrepreneur can present business proposals to the local, state, or federal economic planning boards and directly to the legislators who then can present them to the citizens as a referendum to be voted on. Or, an entrepreneur or group of entrepreneurs can put together a proposition for an initiative , and if they acquire the required signatures, the proposition is presented to the voters as an initiative which is essentially a business plan which will demonstrate and explain its economic viability and how the entrepreneurs, the workers, and the community will profit from this business and how it will serve the common good. If the voters approve the initiative, they have agreed to go into partnership with the entrepreneurs and workers in the business. Also, workers in the private sector can collectively organize and make proposals, often for existing businesses that are being abandoned by capitalist or owners because they are not making enough profit, or the owner is retiring, dies, or is just moving on. All the workers must demonstrate is that the business can cover the cost of the investment, pay the workers a reasonable wage, and provide a service or product that benefits the community, and everyone profits. The banks, planning boards, and research, education, and training centers can also offer their expertise and resources to aid in the revitalization of the business and improve the quality of the product or service. In our system of economic democracy everyone is an entrepreneur, everyone is a worker, everyone is a capitalist and citizen investor, and everyone profits from their investment in each other.

> In order to protect the entrepreneur in our system of economic democracy and make certain that they are rewarded like any artist for their creativity and organizational talents and vision, by law it will be determined that if the legally designated entrepreneur or group of entrepreneurs are pushed out of the business, or, at any time, they decide to leave the business that they created, the citizen investors and the workers must either buy out their royalty rights or pay them a royalty for their entrepreneurial efforts

based on a designated percentage of the gross profit. This is also true of corporations that reach the codetermination threshold of 2000 employees, and the company is converted to a phase one economic democracy. However, as noted above, even though we make certain that the entrepreneur is rewarded for their creative, innovative, and organizational skills, in our system of economic democracy everyone is an entrepreneur, everyone is a worker, everyone is a capitalist and citizen investor, and everyone profits from our investment in each other.

The Market

In our economy, the market is not the master. The market is the servant. Properly regulated and monitored, it is a good barometer to determine the supply and demand for consumer and capital goods and services with significant exceptions, (1) When the American people determine specific products, goods, and services are necessary to the well-being and vitality of the body politic and reflect and nurture the best in all of us, i.e. free high quality education at all levels and free high quality health care for all. (2) When the American people decide to subsidize and support new research, technology, and new industries, products, and services that are critical to our economy and the commonwealth, i.e. renewable and sustainable energy sources, products, services; and the development of a transportation and a utilities system that takes full advantages of these critical investment in the future. (3) Protection against pricing that externalizes the true cost of a product or service, i.e. the true cost to American labor and citizen investors when they have to compete against imports produced by child labor, slave labor, and workers who are not even paid a living wage. (4) Protection against domestic and foreign imported products and services that externalize the cost to the environment and freely pollute. (5) Protection against American corporations and companies that think they can export our industries and jobs and come back into this country with their products and services and not pay a tariff that reflects the true cost to the American people and the host nation. Simply stated, our borders are closed to domestic and foreign vampires looking for blood.

Wage Incentives and Leisure

Incentives in terms of monetary return will be determined by citizens and workers collectively. Given our culture and what we value in terms of how we view success, Americans, even in a regulated market that is filtered through the needs and will of all the American people, will still reward talent, effort, entrepreneurialism, creativity, and all other forms of outstanding contributions to the common good, but these rewards will be more modest and will not reflect the horrific gaps and disparities we see today in incomes and wealth; rather, they will reflect the respect and esteem given to those who contribute the most to the common good; and, at the same time, the individual in all their uniqueness will be nurtured as the source of all creativity, innovation, and meaning.

As for leisure, today in America there is no leisure. As the dynamo of vampire capitalism speeds up using more and more blood to keep itself going, the American people from the bottom up and top down are working longer and faster. For the most part, if we have any extended time off from work, it is not called leisure, it is called unemployment, and we spend that time in misery. What little leisure we have while we are working the thankless, unrewarding, dumb down jobs we have is not leisure. It is an escape into mindless entertainment, alcohol, drugs, and/or digitalized relationships reducing us to one sentence tweets with people we never see, touch, or hug, and our minds are reduced to this. ☺

In our America of political and economic democracy where we directly participate in all the most important decisions that affect our lives, our nation, community, and our livelihood; leisure is not an escape because there is nothing to escape from. Increased leisure is about family, community, self-development, and self-realization, having fun, learning how to play again, and getting back to our dream world where it all began. Basically, we are going to work ourselves out of a job. For example, if we automate a whole industry, we are not unemployed. We all own it. If increasingly more and more Americans have more leisure time to work on what they want to work on, we can assimilate a new wave of immigrants, and they too can become part of the New America as equal partners in our direct and participatory political and economic system. They are no longer the cheap labor of vampire capitalism that is used to keep working Americans divided, fearful, and underpaid.

However, we can only absorb so many people at any one time into the dream of a new America here in the United States, but we can export that dream to our neighbors by going into partnership with the workers in those countries and thereby planting the seeds of prosperity where no one has to go anywhere but home to feed their families. In addition, by exporting our dream for America, we may have planted the seeds to a United States of South America based on the principles of political and economic democracy and a political and economic system of the people, by the people, and for the people. So, as you can see, we have a lot to learn, and we need the educational system to support our dream of a new America and a new world.

Democracy and the University of Life

> "Enlighten the people generally, and tyranny and oppression of body and mind will vanish like evil spirits at the dawn of Days."
> – Thomas Jefferson

In our system of political and economic democracy, at every level workers, consumers, and citizen owners are represented and participating in all decisions involving our economy and political life with the right at all levels to initiate policy and to recall representatives and appointees who do not serve the common good. Supply and demand are filtered through the whole body politic, and economic entrepreneurship and investment in our economy is funded by all of us from above and below. It is an intricate system of checks and balances, debate and discussion, decisions made at all levels of our political and economic life that reflect our wants and needs, the hopes and dreams of all of us. Our political and economic democracy is our university in life and an education and training ground for true democracy.

> Essentially, we will be living the dream and making it real as we go along, knowing that no one of us has the answer and that the answer is with all of us.

Illustration #25

PART SIX: US 2.0

Illustration #26

US 2.0

So, how do we do it? How do we implement a government and an economy of the People, by the People, and for the People? How do we defeat the vampire capitalist and Leviathans that will try to stop us from taking back our country?

I believe that one of the ways that we can do it is by living the dream and creating an alternative United States of America that we will call US 2.0. US 2.0 will be an Internet voting system of direct and participatory democracy where the citizen/members of US 2.0 can initiate "on demand" legislation, reject and demand the repeal of laws passed by their legislatures through the referendum process, and recall representatives and public officials who are not working for us and serving the common good.

This is not an "advisory" initiative, referendum, and recall process. This is an "on demand" process. By this I mean all the citizen/members of US 2.0 will pledge to support the initiative, referendum, and recall process of direct and participatory democracy no matter how they voted on any individual proposition. By support I mean that we are pledged to oppose and campaign against any representative or public official that does not support and work to implement the will of the people. On the other hand, we will support and work for candidates that work for and fight to implement the will of the people as manifested in our "on demand" initiative, referendum, and recall process of direct and participatory democracy. By support, we also mean that candidates for public office and representatives will have to support and work actively for the amendment of city and county charters, state constitutions, and the Constitution of the United States so that the initiative, referendum, and recall process of citizen lawmaking becomes part of the formal voting system.

In cities and states that have the initiative and/or the referendum, and/or recall process in one form or another, we will work to make certain that they have all the instruments of direct democracy, including the right to amend their charters or constitutions. We will also work to eliminate all unreasonable obstacles to the will of the people, i.e. obstructionist signature requirements and time limits; lack of financial, technical, and legal aid; and a platform from which the supporters of a proposition can inform the public, debate, and recruit volunteers. Essentially, we will make the process more accessible to the average American so that we all can do it.

In mirroring our Phase One and Phase Two plan for political and economic democracy in America, US 2.0 will reflect our aspirations for an economy by the people. Our citizen/members will be able to initiate propositions, which will essentially be business proposals, where we the people will go into partnership with American labor and share in the profits mirroring organizationally the formal structure that we described earlier in the study of direct and participatory democracy in the workplace.

US 2.0 will be supported by a university quality information and research base, and we will get to know one another through our forums, blogs, tweets, and our equivalent of face book. We will also get to know one another in real time, in real life beyond our virtual reality network of democracy through social events, gatherings, recreation activities, activism, fairs, festivals, concerts, and mass assemblies where we will celebrate our shared dream of a New America.

The success of US 2.0 depends on us standing as one and honoring our pledge not to be tempted by the taste of blood that the vampire capitalists will offer us. Unity is fundamental to winning the new American revolution and taking back our country, and it is not surprising that the need for unity in the defense of democracy can be traced back to the origins of democracy and how the ancient Athenian Greeks fought their wars. The key to understanding how the Athenians fought and were successful, often against superior number and power, is to be found in the concept of the phalanx.

The phalanx as a battle formation was essentially a moving human wall of shields, a fortress of men eight to ten rows deep or more behind which the Greek citizen soldier fought with spear and sword. If one man fell in the front ranks, another man took his place in the wall. The key to the plan was always to fight as one and never break ranks. The army of Ancient Athens was a citizen army made up of all classes of Athenian society that trained together and fought together as one. Their strength was in their unity, so when it came time to detrmine whether or not they were going to war, they assembled in mass and voted for or against the war by banging their swords against their shields.

This primitive concept of democracy and the power of free will were forged in the fire of battle where blood is blood, and it reached its fullest realization and sophistication in Athens during the Age of Celeistenes and Pericles. In 510 BC, Cleistenes in his struggle with Isagora, a rival aristocrat, promised the Athenians that if they supported him he would institute a democracy in Athens. In the struggle between these two men for supremacy in Athens, Isagora got the support of the Spartans who then by force took control of the Acropolis, the Athenian citadel and seat of power. Believing in Cleistenes promise of democracy, the Athenian people rose up and drove the Spartans out in what was the first democratic revolution in history. However, it was during the Age of Pericles that democracy reached its zenith.

Under Pericles, all Athenian male citizens eighteen years and older were freed to participate equally in the Athenian state. The General Assembly, which was comprised of all the male citizens of Athens, became the law making body of direct and participatory democracy where each and every citizen had the right to debate, initiate, repeal, and pass laws for the community and these laws applied to every one equally. The most important executive funtions of the state were conducted by a representative people's council of five hundred citizens chosen by lot, fifty from each of the politcal and defense units that Celeistheses created. Most public officials and administrators of the government and civil servants were also chosen by lot as were the jurers in legal cases. In the trials, there were no lawyers and the accused and the accuser had to argue their own case in front of the jurers.

Athens, it was estimated, had a population of appdroximately 200,000 people at its peak, and democracy thrived in Athens for approximately one hundred and fifty years before its demise with the defeat of Athens by the Spartans and its allies in the Second Peloponnesian War of 431-404BC. What Athens was to the Athenian people was probably best expressed by Pericles in a funeral oration in honor of the Athenians who had fought and died for their city during the Spartan Wars.

Illustration #27

Our form of government does not enter into rivalry with the institutions of others. Our government does not copy our neighbors but is an example to them. It is true that we are called a democracy, for the administration is in the hands of the many and not of the few. But while there exists equal justice to all and alike in their private disputes, the claim of excellence is also recognized, and when a citizen is in any way distinguished, he is preferred to the public service, not as a matter of privilege, but as the reward of merit. Neither is poverty an obstacle, but a man may benefit his country whatever the obscurity of his condition. There is no exclusiveness in our public life and in our private business. We are not suspicious of one another, nor angry with our neighbor if he does what he likes; we do not put on sour looks at him which, though harmless, are not pleasant. While we are thus unconstrained in our private business, a spirit of reverence pervades our public acts; we are prevented from doing wrong by respect for the authorities and for the laws, having a particular regard to those which are ordained for the protection of the injured as well as those unwritten laws which bring upon the transgressor of them the reprobation of the general sentiment. – Excerpt from Pericles Funeral Oration as recorded for posterity by Thucydides

Five hundred years later, Plutarch saw the city that Pericles and the Athenian's built and wrote, "Such is the bloom of perpetual newness, as it were, upon these works of his, which makes them ever to look untouched by time, as though the unflattering breath of an ageless spirit had been infused into them."

In the short period that Athens thrived, this moderately sized city by contemporary standards, became the birthplace of Western Civilization in politics, philosophy, architecture, arts, drama, history, mathematics, and science, and its spirit is very much alive two thousand five hundred years later. Our concept of beauty came from the aesthetics and artistic standards of the great Athenian artists Myron, Orates, Praxiteles, Phidias and the architects Ictinus, Lakatos, and Karpion. Our literary, linguistic, and dramatic forms came directly from the linguistic and dramatic analysis of Aristotle and the literary and dramatic form created by Aeschylus, Aristophanes, Euripides, and Sophocles. Logical analysis, philosophy, and the scientific approach was born in the minds of Aristotle, Plato, Socrates, Pythagoras, Democritus, and Archimedes as was the mathematical mysteries of reality hidden in Euclid's geometry of nature. Ancient Greek mythology has been an inspiration to modern poets and psychologists to the point that we could say that Freud merely translated the great myths and Greek dramas into modern terms.

Amidst all this greatness, however, probably their greatest achievement was the fact that they discovered the Idea of an Idea. From that Idea all ideas were born and flourished, and one of the greatest ideas that they created was the idea of democracy that tragically died with the Golden Age of Ancient Athens. We would not see that idea again until the American Revolution of the 1770s and the taking of the Bastille on July 14, 1789 that started the French Revolution, and even then and now we have experienced only a shadow of the greatness of that spirit. However, today we are at the threshold of a New Golden Age of Democracy, but we are going to have to fight for it, and the question once again becomes the question that was asked at the origins of democracy when the Ancient Athenian citizen soldiers stood at the front ranks of an idea and a vision of immortality. What are we fighting for?

A Vision for America

True democracy recognizes and cherishes the uniqueness of each and every one of us. It recognizes that there will never be anyone like you or me ever again. No one will ever again quite see the world from our point of view, right here, right now, where we stand or sit or lie or run or weep or cry or laugh with joy at the magnificence and the horror of it all. We are the secret. We are the mystery.

When quantum physics probes the essence of the universe, it is probing the essence of the human mind and spirit. The universe is not something out there. It is within us, and it is that mystery, that infinite creativity, that quantum universe at the heart of you and me that makes us human, makes us unique, make us precious; and, at the same time, makes us everything that ever was and will be. We are the mystery. We are the secret; and collectively, We the People are the spirit that transcends each of us alone.

It is this spirit that reveals itself when we are at one with ourselves, at one with each other, and at one with the world around us. It is this spirit that reveals itself in family, friends, community, and country. It is this spirit that embraces the global family. It is this spirit at the heart of the universe. It is the spirit of love, the one word that is the key to the Gates of a New Eden and the nexus of the universe around which all else revolves. This is the lesson of true democracy. This is the essence of *The New American Revolution.* This is the lesson we must learn, or we will die.

Illustration #28

Coming Home

Work Cited

1. Bachrach, Peter, Aryeh Botwinick, *Power and Empowerment: A radical Theory of Participatory Democracy*, Temple University Press, Philadelphia 1992
2. Barber, Benjamin, Strong Democracy: Participatory Politics for a New Age, University of California Press, Los Angeles 1984
3. Bowler, Shaun, Todd Donovan, *Demanding Choices,* University of Michigan Press Ann Arbor, MI, 1994
4. Campbell, John Franklin, 'The Death Rattle of the American Establishment," New York, September 20, 1971
5. CBS News/New York Time Poll, View of the Parties, July 11-15, 2004 CBS/New York Times Poll, July 11-15, 2004 https://www.cbsnews.com/htdocs/CBSNews_polls/parties_views.pdf
6. Clay, Calvert "Freedom of Speech Extended to Corporations." 2000, cited from Finkleman, Paul, Encyclopedia of America Civil Liberties, Vol 1 CRC Press
7. Coghlan, Andy and Debora MacKenzie, "Revealed – The Capitalist Network That Runs the World", New Scientist, 19 October 2011, https://www.newscientist.com/aticle/mg21228354.-500-reveal-the-capital-network-that-runs-the-world/
8. Cohen, Paul, "Lessons from the Nationalization Nation: State-Owned Enterprises in France," Dissent Magazine, Winter 2010 https://www.dissentmagazine.org/article/lessons-from-the-nationalization-nation-state-owned-enterprises-in-france
9. Collins, Chuck and Felice Yeskel, Economic *Apartheid in America: A Primer in Economic Inequality and Insecurity*, New Press, New York, 2005,
10. Confessore, Michael, "*Koch Brothers' Budget of $889 million for 2016 Is on Par With Both Parties' Spending,"* New York Times, Jan 26, 2015 http://www.nytimes.com/2015/01/27/us/politics/Koch-plan-to-spend-900-million-on-2016-campaign/
11. Dubois, Philip, Floyd Feeney, and Edmund Constantine 1991, *The California Ballot Pamphlet: A Survey of Voters: Report Prepared for the Office of the Secretary of the State of California*, March 1991
12. Duff, Gordon, "Suppressed History: When Wall Street Tried to Bring the Holocaust to America. Veterans Today, October 13, 2010 https://www.veteranstodayarchives.com/2010/10/13/suppressed-history-hidden-facts-behind-the-wall-street-nazi-plot/
13. Easterbrook, Greg, "Myth of Oppressive Corporate Taxes," The Atlantic Online, June 1982 https://www.theatlantic.com/past/docs/politics/ecbig/ececoeas.htm
14. Furman, Jason, Prepared Testimony for the Hearing "Disappearing Corporate Income Tax," U.S House of Representatives Committee on Ways and Means, February 11, 2020 https://www.piie.com/system/files/documents/furman2020-02-11.pdf
15. Gates, Jeff, *Democracy at Risk: Rescuing Main Street from Wall Street*, Perseus Publishing, Cambridge, Mass 2001
16. Gerber, Elizabeth, *Interest Group Influence in the California Initiative Process*, Public Policy Institute of California
17. Gerber, Elizabeth, *The Popular Paradox: Interest Group Influence and he Promise of Direct Democracy,* Princeton University Press, 1999
18. Greenwood, Daphine and Edward Wolf, "Changes in wealth in the United States 1962-1983, Journal of Population economics, 1992

19. Grieder, William, *Secrets of the Temple: How the Federal Reserve Runs the Country*, Touchstone Books Published by Simon & Schuster, New York 1998
20. Gross, Bertram, *Friendly Fascism: The New Face of Power in America*, South End Press, 2008
21. Gunnell, Barbara, "The Great Bura Irrigation Scheme Disaster," African Business April 1986
22. Hahn, Jonah, "*The Degrading Force of Money in Politics*," Harvard Political Review, October 20, 2015, http://ww.harvardpolitics.com/unitedstates/the-degrading-force-of-money-in-politics/
23. Hajnal, Zoltan, Hugh Louch, *Are There Winners and Losers? Race, Ethnicity, and California's Initiative Process*, Public Policy Institute of California
24. Harvey, David, *The Enigma of Capital: And the Crisis of Capitalism*, Oxford University Press, New York 2010
25. Ingraham, "Christopher, *Somebody Just Put a Price Tag on the 2016 Election. It's* a Doozy," The Washington Post, http://www.washingtonpost.com/news/wonk/wp/2017/04/14/somebody-just-put-a-price-tag-on-the-2016-election-its-a-doozy
26. Institute on Taxation and Economic Policy https://itep.org/corporate-tax-avoidance-in-the-first-year-of-the-rump-tax-laws
27. Kelly, Marjorie, *The Devine Right of Capital: Dethroning the Corporate Aristocracy*, Berret-Koehler Publishers Inc., San Francisco2001,2003
28. Keyssar, Alexander, The Right to Vote: The Contested History of Democracy in the United State, Basic Books, New York 2000
29. Kotlifoff, Lawrence and Lawrence Summers, "The Role of Intergenerational Transfers in Aggregate Capital Accumulation", Journal of Political Economy 1981
30. Krupp, Alfried, 1933-1945- "Krupp Under the Nazis," Global Security Organization,https://www.globalsecurity.org/military/world/europe/krupp-08.htm
31. Krupp, Alfried von Bohlen und Halback, Wikipedia, https://en.wikipedia.org/wiki/Alfried_Krupp_von_Bohlen_und_Halbach
32. Long, Will, "*How Much Money Are We Pouring into Elections?" http://followmyvote.com/money-in-politics-facts/*
33. Making Change at Walmart, Commercial Workers International Union (UFCW) http://www.changewalmart.org
34. Magleby, David, *Direct Legislation: Voting on Ballot Propositions in the United States*, John Hopkins University Press, Baltimore, MD, 1984
35. McChesney, Robert W., *The New Global Media; It's a Small World of Big Conglomerates,* The Nation Magazine, November 29, 1999 http://www.hartfordhwp.com/archives/29/053.html
36. Merelli, Annalisa, "*The US Has A Lot of Money, But It Does Not Look Like a Developed Country*," Quartz, March 10, 2017 https://www.qz.com/879092/the-us-doesn't-look-like-a-developed-country/
37. Noah, Timothy, "The Mobility Myth," The New Republic, Feb 8, 2012. http://newrepublic.com/article/How the Federal Reserve Runs 100516/inequality-mobility-economics-america-recession-divergence accessed 8/21/2018
38. Norton, Michael I., Dan Ariely, "Spreading the Wealth" Los Angeles Times, Nov.8,2010, https://www.latimes.com/archives/la-xpm-2010-nov-08-la-oe-norton-wealth-inequality-20101108-story.html
39. Peet, Richard, Unholy Trinity: The IMF, World Bank, and WTO, Zed Books, New York 2010

40. Piper, Bill Piper *"A Brief Analysis of Vote Behavior Regarding Tax Initiative From 1928 to March 2000,* a study sponsored by the Initiative and Referendum Institute, Citizen Lawmakers Press, Washington, DC
41. Renteln, Theodor Adrian von, Wikipedia, https://en.wikipedia.org/wiki/Adrian_von_Renteln
42. Ripple, William J., Christopher Wolf, Thomas M. Newsome, Mauro Galetti, Mohammed Alamgir, Eileen Crist, Mahmoud I. Mahmoud, William F. Laurance, 15,364 scientists signatories from 184 countries, "World Scientists' Warning to Humanity: A Second Notice, BioScience, Volume 67, Issue 12, December 2017 https://doi.org/10.1093/biosci/bix125
43. Sabato, Larry, Howard Ernst, Bruce *A. Larson, Dangerous Democracy? The Battle Over Ballot Initiatives in America,* Rowman & Littlefield Publishers, Inc, Hanham 2001
44. Secret Meeting of 20 February 1933, https://en.wikipedia.org/wiki/Secret_Meeting_of_20_February_1933
45. Schweickart, David, *After Capitalism*, Bowman & Littlefield Publishes, Inc. Lanham, 2002
46. Spector, Dina, "18 Facts About Walmart That Will low Your Mind," Business Insider, Nov. 15, 2012, https://www.businessinsider.com/crazy-facts-about-walmart-2012-11)
47. Terborgh, John, "The World Is In Overshoot," The New York Review of Books, December 3, 2009 https://www.nybooks.com/articles/2009/12/03/the-world-is-in-overshoot/
48. Tyler, George, The Codetermination Difference, American Prospect: Ideas, Politics & Power, January 10, 2019 https://prospect.org/labor/codetermination-difference/
49. United States Supreme Court, 118US 394 (1886) Santa Clara v Southern Pacific
50. United States Supreme Court, 125 US 1888 Pembina Consolidated Silver Mining Co v Pennsylvania
51. Vogler, Albert, Wikipedia, https://en.wikipedia.org/wiki/Albert_Vögler
52. Wachtel, H., 1998, "Labor's State in the WTO", American Prospect, March/April 1998
53. World Bank, https://www.worldbank.org/

References

1. Alperovitz, Gar, *America Beyond Capitalism: Reclaiming Our Wealth, Our Liberty, and Our Democracy, John* Wiley & Sons Inc., Hoboken 2005
2. Bakan, Joel, The Corporation: The Pathological Pursuit of Profit and Power, Free Press 2005
3. Burbach, Roger, Orlando Nunez and Boris Kagarilitsky, *Globalization and Its Discontents: The Rise of Postmodern Socialisms,* Pluto Press, London 1997
4. Cage, Julia, *Saving the Media*, Translated by Arthur Goldhammer, The Belknap Press of Harvard University Press, Cambridge, 2015
5. Friedman, Milton, *Capitalism and Freedom,* The University of Chicago Press, Chicago 1962
6. Grieber, William, *One World, Ready or Not: The Manic Logic of Global Capitalism,* Touchstone Books, New York 1998
7. Greiber, William, *Who Will Tell the People: The Betrayal of American Democracy,* Touchstone Books, New York 1993
8. Griffin, Edward G., *The Creature from Jekyll Island, 5th edition,* American Media, West Lake Village 2010

9. Hackett, Robert A., William K. Carroll, *Remaking Media: The Struggle to Democratize Public Communication,* Routledge, Taylor, & Francis Group, New York 2006

10. Hahnel, Robin, *The ABCs of Political Economy,* Pluto Press, London 2000

11. Hahnel, Robin, *Economic Justice and Democracy: From Competition to Cooperation,* Routledge, Taylor & Francis, New York 2005

12. Hind, Dan, *The Return of the Public: Democracy, Power, and the Case for Media Reform,* Verso, London 2012

13. Johnson, Chalmers, *The Sorrows of Empire: Militarism, Secrecy, and the End of the Republic,* A Metropolitan/Owl Book, Henry Holt & Co., New York 2005

14. Korten, David C. *When Corporations Rule the World,* second edition, A Co-publication of Kumarian Press, Inc. and Berrett-Koehler Publishers, Inc., San Francisco `1996

15. Kuttner, Robert, *Everything for Sale: The Virtue and Limits of Markets,* A Century Foundation Book, The University of Chicago Press, 1997

16. Miller, James, *Can Democracy Work? A Short History of a Radical Idea: From Ancient Athens to Our World,* Farrar, Straus, & Giroux, New York 2018

17. Perloff, James, *The Shadows of Power: The Council on Foreign Relations and the American Decline,* Western Islands, Appleton 1988

18. Peterson, Wallace, C., *Silent Depression: Twenty-five Years of Wage Squeeze and Middle -Class Decline, W.W. Norton & Company, New York 1995*

19. Philips, Kevin, *Boiling Point: Democrats, Republicans, And the Decline of Middle-Class Prosperity,* Random House, New York 1993

20. Tabb, William K., *The Amoral Elephant: Globalization and the Struggle for Social Justice in the Twenty-First Century,* Monthly Review Press, New York 2001

21. Whyte, William Foote, Kathleen King Whyte, *Making Mondragon: The Growth and Dynamics of the Worker Cooperative Complex,* ILR Press, Ithaca 1988

22. Wolff, Richard, *Democracy at Work: A Cure for Capitalism,* Haymaker Books, Chicago 2012

23. Wolff, Richard in Conversation with David Barsamian, *Occupy the Economy: Challenging Capitalism,* Open Media Series, City Light Books, San Francisco 2012

24. Wolin, Sheldon S., *Democracy Inc.: Managed Democracy and the Specter of Inverted Totalitarianism,* Princeton University Press, Princeton 2012

25. Zimmerman, Joseph F., *Participatory Democracy: Populism Revised,* Praeger, New York 1986

26. Zweig, Michael, *The Working-Class Majority: America's Best Kept Secret,* ILR Press, Ithaca 2000

Charts

1. Chart #1, Social Mobility in the United States, https://www.bong.com/images/search?-infographic+credit+carla+schaffer%2Faaas&qpvt=(nfographic+credit%3a+Carla+Schffe%2fAAAS)&form=IGRE&first=1&cw=1377&ch=577

2. Chart #2, Economic Backgrounds of Students at 146 Colleges, America's Untapped Resources: Low income Students in Higher Education, https://www.bing.com/images/search?view=detailV2&insightstoken=bcid_SGMI7hassikB17PO33l1dZBPxrtn.....yl*ccid_wjuFqyy&form=SBIHMP&iss=SBIUPLOADGET&sbisrc=ImgPaste&idpbck=1&sbifsz=360+x+270+%c2%b7+17.76+kB+%c2%b7+png&sbifnm=image.png&thw=360&thh=270&ptime=34&dlen=24248&expw=360&exph=270&selectedindex=0&id=-960727073&ccid=YwjuFqyy&vt=2&sim=11
3. Chart #3, Share of National Income by Class, Source: Data from DENavas-Walt C. Proctor, B.D., & Smith, J.C. (2010). Income, poverty, and health insurance coverage in the United States: 2009 (Annual Population Report P60-238) Washington, DC: U.S. Census Bureau. https://socialsci.libretexts.org/Bookshelves/Sociology/Book:_Sociology_(Barkan)/06:_Social_Stratification/6.05:_Economic_Inequality_and_Poverty_in_the_United_States
4. Chart #4, Ranking of the United States in Income Inequality, (Source: Data from Michel, L., Bernstein, J., & Shierholz, H. (2009) The state of working America 2008/2009, Ithaca, N.Y.: ILR Press [an imprint of Cornell University Press].) https://socialsci.libretexts.org/Bookshelves/Sociology/Book:_Sociology_(Barkan)/06:_Social_Stratification/6.05:_Economic_Inequality_and_Poverty_in_the_United_StatesChart #5,
5. The Distribution of Financial Wealth in the United States, Graphic is based on research by The Levy Institution which uses data from the Federal Reserve Board, http://www.upwrthy.com/a-fugly-tuth-made-pretty-a-cartoonists-depiction-of-wealth-inequality-ma3-5f
6. Chart #6, If Us Land Was Divided Like US Wealth, Graphic is based on research by The Levy Institution which uses data from the Federal Reserve Board, http://www.upwrthy.com/a-fugly-tuth-made-pretty-a-cartoonists-depiction-of-wealth-inequality-ma3-5f
7. Chart #6, Comparison of an Actual, Estimated, and Ideal Distribution of Wealth, On Logus, "*The Imaginary Middle Class," Dec. 18, 2019, https://onlogos.wordpress.com/*
8. Chart #8, Facts About Walmart, Source Andy Kroll, Mother Jones, March/April 2012 issue, https://www.motherjones.com/environment/2012/03/walmart-sales-energy-use-statistics
9. Chart #9, Global Reach, Andy Coghlan and Debora MacKenzie, *"Revealed The Capitalist Network That Runs the World,"* New Scientist, 19 October 2011, http://www.newscientist.ocm/article/mg21228354.-500-reveal-the-capital-network-that-runs-the-world
10. Chart #10, The Blood Bank, https://www.bing.com/images/search?view=detailV2&insightstoken=bcid_
11. vyLa3wXikB17PO33l1dZBPxrtn.....8Q*ccid_O%2FItrfBe&form=S-BIHMP&iss=SBIUPLOADGET&sbisrc=ImgPaste&idpbck=1&s-bifsz=449+x+821+%c2%b7+45.75+kB+%c2%b7+png&sbifnm=image.png&thw=449&thh=821&ptime=69&dlen=62460&expw=443&exph=811&selectedindex=0&id=755661188&ccid=O%2FItrfBe&vt=2&sim=11
12. Chart #11, The Impending Disappearance of the World's Natural Resources Source: www.geois.de/?p=2055
13. Chart #12, Swing States, Odyssey, *Understanding the Electoral College*, by Mary Abrahamyan, Northeastern University, Aug 10,2016 https://www.theodysseyonline.com/understanding-electoral-college-101

14. Chart #13, One-Dollar-One-Vote, Thinking Oregon, Hillary Money Grab by W. Machen, September 27, 2016 http://www.thinkingoregon.org/2016/09/27/down-the-memory-hole-hillarys-commitment-to-limiting-influence-of-big-money-on -politics

15. Chart #14, Initiative Passage and Failure Rate, Gerber, Elizabeth, The Popular Paradox: Interest Group Influence & the Promise of Direct Democracy, Princeton University Press 17-18

16. Chart #15, Popularity of Initiative, PPIC Statewide Survey, January 2000 Are *There Winners and Losers? Race Ethnicity, and California's Initiative Process,* by Zoltan Hajnal and Hugh Louch, Public Policy Institute, California, 2001, p 45.

17. Chart #16, Percentage Voting for the Winning Side, *Are There Winners and Losers? Race Ethnicity, and California's Initiative Process,* by Zoltan Hajnal and Hugh Louch, Public Policy Institute, California, 2001, p 46

18. Chart #17, Income Tax Rates for 379 Companies, 2018, :Institute on Taxation and Economic Policy analysis of corporate 10-K filings

19. Chart #18, Historical Highest Marginal Income Tax Rate, PBS News Hour, *Save the Pensions: Tax the Rich*, by Paul Solman, Feb, 28, 2011, (Source – table from Tax Policy Center of the Urban Institute and Brookings Institution) https://www.pbs.org/newshour/economy/save-the-pensions-tax-the-rich

Illustrations

1. Illustration #1, Vampires are Real, Tino, Marcello and Andrea Dalla Bona, *Learn or Die: The New American Revolution*, Thompson and Prince 2020

2. Illustration #2, Aztec Sacrifice, An image taken from the Codex Mendoza, created by native scribes for the Spanish in 1541-1542, showing a ritual Aztec www.aztec-history.com/aztec-sacrifice.html

3. Illustration #3, Trickle Down Blood, Gross, Bertram, *Friendly Fascism: The New Face of Power in America, South End Press, Boston, 1980*

4. Illustration #4, Paradise Mall, Tino, Marcello and Andrea Dalla Bona, *Learn or Die: The New American Revolution*, Thompson and Prince 2020

5. Illustration #5, Knowledge is Power, Tino, Marcello and Andrea Dalla Bona, *Learn or Die: The New American Revolution*, Thompson and Prince 2020

6. Illustration #6, I Never Thought It Was This Bad, Tino, Marcello and Andrea Dalla Bona, *Learn or Die: The New American Revolution*, Thompson and Prince 2020

7. Illustration #7, So Where Does This God Dwell? Tino, Marcello and Andrea Dalla Bona, *Learn or Die: The New American Revolution,* Thompson and Prince 2020

8. Illustration #8, Aztec Sacrifice, An image taken from the Codex Mendoza, created by native scribes for the Spanish in 1541-1542, showing a ritual Aztec www.aztec-history.com/aztec-sacrifice.html

9. Illustration #9, Hiroshima Then and Now, Tino, Marcello and Andrea Dalla Bona, *Learn or Die: The New American Revolution*, Thompson and Prince 2020

10. Illustration #10, The Leviathan, Tino, Marcello and Andrea Dalla Bona, *Learn or Die: The New American Revolution*, Thompson and Prince 2020

11. Illustration #11, WB, WTO, & IMF, Tino, Marcello and Andrea Dalla Bona, *Learn or Die: The New American Revolution*, Thompson and Prince 2020
12. Illustration #12, We're Committing Suicide, Tino, Marcello and Andrea Dalla Bona, *Learn or Die: The New American Revolution*, Thompson and Prince 2020
13. Illustration #13, Journey's End I, Tino, Marcello and Andrea Dalla Bona, *Learn or Die: The New American Revolution*, Thompson and Prince 2020Illustration #14, Journey's End II, Tino, Marcello and Andrea Dalla Bona, *Learn or Die: The New American Revolution*, Thompson and Prince 2020
14. Illustration #14, Journey's End II, Tino, Marcello and Andrea Dalla Bona, *Learn or Die: The New American Revolution*, Thompson and Prince 2020
15. Illustration #15, They Sold Us Out, Tino, Marcello and Andrea Dalla Bona, *Learn or Die: The New American Revolution*, Thompson and Prince 2020
16. Illustration #16, Power to the People, Tino, Marcello and Andrea Dalla Bona, *Learn or Die: The New American Revolution*, Thompson and Prince 2020
17. Illustration #17, The Illusion of Choice, Tino, Marcello and Andrea Dalla Bona, *Learn or Die: The New American Revolution*, Thompson and Prince 2020
18. Illustration #18, The Alchemy of Money, Tino, Marcello and Andrea Dalla Bona, *Learn or Die: The New American Revolution*, Thompson and Prince 2020
19. Illustration#19, Who Is in This Picture? Tino, Marcello and Andrea Dalla Bona, *Learn or Die: The New American Revolution*, Thompson and Prince 2020
20. Illustration #20, New York Times, All That's Interesting, https://allthatsinteresting.com/the-business-plot
21. Illustration #21, General Smedley Butler, Fascist Plot to Seize Government by Force, ATI, *The Business Plot: The Little-Known Story of the Wall Street Scheme to Launch a Fascist Coup in A America by Andrew Lenoir, September 2, 019* http://allthatsinteresting.com/the-business-plot
22. Illustration #22, Is It Happening Now? Tino, Marcello and Andrea Dalla Bona, *Learn or Die: The New American Revolution*, Thompson and Prince 2020
23. Illustration #23, Democracy Doesn't Stop at The Workplace Door, Tino, Marcello and Andrea Dalla Bona, *Learn or Die: The New American Revolution*, Thompson and Prince 2020
24. Illustration #24, What About Them? Now? Tino, Marcello and Andrea Dalla Bona, *Learn or Die: The New American Revolution*, Thompson and Prince 2020
25. Illustration #25, This Way To US.2.0, Tino, Marcello and Andrea Dalla Bona, *Learn or Die: The New American Revolution*, Thompson and Prince 2020
26. Illustration #26, US 2.0, Tino, Marcello and Andrea Dalla Bona, *Learn or Die: The New American Revolution*, Thompson and Prince 2020
27. Illustration #27, Pericles, Tino, Marcello and Andrea Dalla Bona, *Learn or Die: The New American Revolution*, Thompson and Prince 2020
28. Illustration #28, Going Home, Tino, Marcello and Andrea Dalla Bona, *Learn or Die: The New American Revolution*, Thompson and Prince 2020

About the Author

"We are everything that ever was or will be. Yet, each and every one of us is totally unique, never, ever, to be seen again. *We are the mystery at the heart of the universe.* That is what we are all about."

Marcello

Made in United States
North Haven, CT
24 September 2026

19102542R00075